PRIMARY

AUTHOR
MIGUEL KAGAN

ART & DESIGN
ALEX CORE
CELSO RODRIGUEZ
MILES RICHEY
DENISE ALPHABET

EDITOR
KATHY TOMLINSON

PUBLISHER
KAGAN PUBLISHING

33234000424230

R. L. LONGSTREET MEDIA CENTER

© 2002 by *Kagan Publishing*

This book is published and distributed by *Kagan Publishing*. All rights are reserved by *Kagan Publishing*. No part of this publication may be reproduced or transmitted in any form by any means, electronic or mechanical, including photocopy, recording, or any information storage and retrieval system, without prior written permission from *Kagan Publishing*. The blackline masters and card sets included in this book may be duplicated only by classroom teachers who purchase the book, and only for use in their own classrooms. To obtain additional copies of this book, other products by *Kagan Publishing*, or information regarding professional development, contact *Kagan Publishing*.

Kagan Publishing

981 Calle Amanecer

San Clemente, CA 92673

(949) 545-6300

Fax: (949) 545-6301

1 (800) 933-2667

www.KaganOnline.com

ISBN: 978-1-879097-73-5

TABLE OF
CONTENTS

INTRODUCTION

Transform content mastery into a fun and energizing learning game. Your students will enjoy mixing and quizzing each other so much, they won't even notice how much information they're learning. Mix-N-Match is a great classbuilding activity too. Students are out of their seats, having fun, and learning with all classmates.

HOW TO PLAY

On the following pages, you'll find step-by-step instructions. Here's a nutshell description of Mix-N-Match: Students each receive a Mix-N-Match card. They stand up and pair up. Students each quiz their partner, then get quizzed by their partner, then trade cards. They repeatedly quiz, quiz, and trade, each time with a new partner. Finally, the teacher has them find their partner with the matching card.

There are numerous additional learning games you can play with the Mix-N-Match cards in this book. We'll get to those in a few pages.

WHEN TO PLAY

The 12 Mix-N-Match sets in this book were designed to help students master basic information and skills. Pull out the corresponding Mix-N-Match set when you're studying a topic. The cards are great for acquiring the content and for review. If the content on the cards is new content for your students, it is recommended that you introduce the content before they play.

One word of caution: Content mastery is important, but it's just one part of the entire educational picture. These sets were designed to supplement other great things you do in your classroom: the investigations, the projects, the discussions... They are not intended to replace them!

WHAT'S IN THIS BOOK

INTRO PAGE

Each Mix-N-Match set has an intro page. On the intro page are "Quizzing Questions." These are questions you can have students ask each other as they quiz their partners using their cards.

MIX-N-MATCH

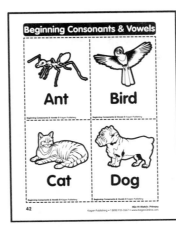

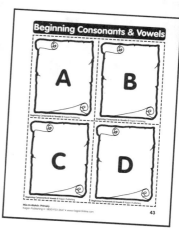

WORKSHEETS

Following the intro page, there are two reproducible worksheets associated with each Mix-N-Match set. These worksheets can be used to practice the concepts before playing Mix-N-Match or for reinforcing the concepts after Mix-N-Match.

You can use a variety of Kagan structures for the worksheets, or even have students work independently. We recommend you use the RallyCoach structure to have students do the problems on the worksheet. For RallyCoach, students pair up. Partner A solves the first problem while Partner B watches, checks, and praises or coaches. For the next problem, Partner B solves the problem while Partner A watches, checks, and praises or coaches. Partners take turns solving each problem. This structure allows students to watch how their peers solve problems and allows for peer tutoring when necessary.

MIX-N-MATCH CARDS

Next, and at the heart of the book are the Mix-N-Match Cards. On each two-page spread, you will find the matching cards so it is easy to see at a glance which cards are a "match." The card in the upper left corner on the even page matches the card in the upper left corner on the odd page.

ANSWER PAGE

On the last page of each card set, there is an answer page. On this page, you will either find the answers to all the matches in the card set, the answers to the worksheet, or additional helpful information for students. You can use these pages to check students' answers or when introducing or reviewing the matching content.

MIX-N-MATCH

Students mix, repeatedly quizzing new partners and trading cards. Afterward, they rush to find a partner with the card that matches theirs.

MIX-N-MATCH

SET-UP

Copy a Mix-N-Match card set for your class. Cut out the cards, or have students cut out the cards. Distribute the cards so each students receives one card.

STEPS

1 STUDENTS STANDUP–HANDUP–PAIRUP

With a card in their hands, students stand up, push in their chairs, and put their hands up. They keep a hand up until they find a partner. Students use the card to quiz their partners. For example, for the Beginning Consonants and Vowels set, the student with the animal card asks, "What letter do I begin with?"

2 STUDENTS QUIZ PARTNERS

The partner answers. If correct, the partner receives a compliment ("Excellent job!" "Great work!"), or a high five. If incorrect or no answer is given, the partner is given the answer and coached how to remember it.

3 SWITCH ROLES: STUDENTS QUIZ PARTNERS

The other partner quizzes, then praises or coaches. For example, the student with the letter card asks, "What is an animal that begins with this letter?"

4 PARTNERS TRADE CARDS

Partners trade cards and say, "thank you," or "good-bye."

5 REPEAT WITH NEW PARTNERS

Partners split up and repeat Steps 1 through 4 a number of times, repeatedly quizzing new partners and being quizzed by new partners.

6 TEACHER CALLS "FREEZE"

After numerous pairings and ample quizzing time, call, "freeze."

7 STUDENTS FREEZE

Students freeze, look at their cards, and think of their match.

8 STUDENTS FIND THEIR MATCH

Students move to the center of the room, find their match, and quickly move away from the center of the room with their new partner.

EXTENSION

Once students are around the room in pairs, have them each quickly share their match. For our example, one student says, "Dog...," and his or her partner states the match, "begins with the letter 'D.'"

QUIZ, QUIZ, TRADE

MANAGEMENT TIPS

COLOR CODE CARDS

Copy the cards onto two different color card stock papers. Use one color for the cards on even page numbers, and a different color for the cards on odd page numbers. This way, you can easily tell the cards apart.

LAMINATE CARDS

Laminate your card sets to make them more attractive and last for years.

COLLECTING CARDS

When you collect the cards from your students, have them return them in pairs. This will save you lots of time: you get the cards back ready to use the next time.

STORE SETS

Put your card set into an envelope for next time. Each set has a title bar that you cut off when you cut out the cards. Tape that title to the front of your envelope. Or store sets using a rubber band or binder clip.

Numbers and Dots

CARD PAIRS

Each card has a matching card. When distributing the cards, make sure you distribute them in pairs. If you have an extra student, you can either have that student be a "twin" with another student, or you can join in.

MORE STUDENTS THAN CARDS

Card sets are designed for up to 40 students. If you have more than 40 students, make extra copies of the card pairs you'd most like to have students work on. This way, each student gets a card and students practice the desired content more frequently.

PARTIAL SET

If students are having difficulty with specific matching cards, make multiple copies of those cards and have students play Mix-N-Match with this partial set for repeated practice. A partial set is also helpful if there are some cards beyond students' ability level.

Mix-N-Match
Kagan Publishing • 1 (800) 933-2667 • www.KaganOnline.com

HAND UP

Have students put their hands up as soon as they're ready to find a new partner, and put them down as soon as they've found a partner. This makes it easy for students to find partners. If you see a student avoiding another student with his/her hand up, stop the class and remind them to always pair with the nearest person with a hand up.

HIGH FIVE

Students have their hands up when searching for a partner. Have students give each other a high five, then greet each other with a handshake or a friendly greeting ("Hey, buddy") before they quiz each other. This adds to the excitement of the game.

EXAGGERATED PRAISERS

Another thing you can do spice up Mix-N-Match is use exaggerated praisers. Have students use funny compliments that are a little overboard but make us feel good, nevertheless. For example, "That's correct. You must have been awarded at least a dozen Nobel prizes."

NO REPEATS

Tell students that they cannot pair up with the same partner twice.

NOBODY KNOWS

If neither partner knows the answer to a card, have them write it down on a designated area of the chalkboard. The resulting list is a great way to see which cards students need more work on.

MAKE IT A RACE

Record how long it takes students to find their matching partners. Do it repeatedly and see if students can get quicker and beat their previous times.

MAKE YOUR OWN SETS

This book contains 12 ready-to-use sets based on popular topics. It'll provide hours of fun and learning. If you'd like more sets, you can easily create your own Mix-N-Match sets. All you need is matching content. Problems and answers work well. Words and their definitions are also popular.

MORE STRUCTURES

The card sets in this book were designed for Mix-N-Match. But you can also use them with a number of other Kagan Structures...

NUMBERED HEADS TOGETHER

In teams, students number off. Select a card and ask students a question based on the content of the card. Have each student independently write his/her own answer on a sheet of paper or response board. Then, students put their heads together to make sure everyone on their team knows the answer. Call a number and have students with that number share their team's answer.

FLASHCARD GAME

Flashcard Game is based on repeated practice and proceeds through three rounds from the most cues to the least.

Students have a stack of cards they need to practice and a list of correct answers. The student (the tutee) gives his/her cards and answers to a partner (the tutor). The tutor shows the tutee the card and reads the answer. Next, the tutor shows the tutee the card and the tutee answers. If correct, the tutee wins the card back. If wrong, the tutor gives the tutee the correct answer and returns the card to the stack. Once the tutee wins all his/her cards, they proceed to Round 2. In Round 2, the tutor shows the tutee the card and the tutee answers. Once the tutee wins all his/her cards in Round 2, the pair proceeds to Round 3. In Round 3, the tutor does not show the card. He or she reads the card and the tutee answers.

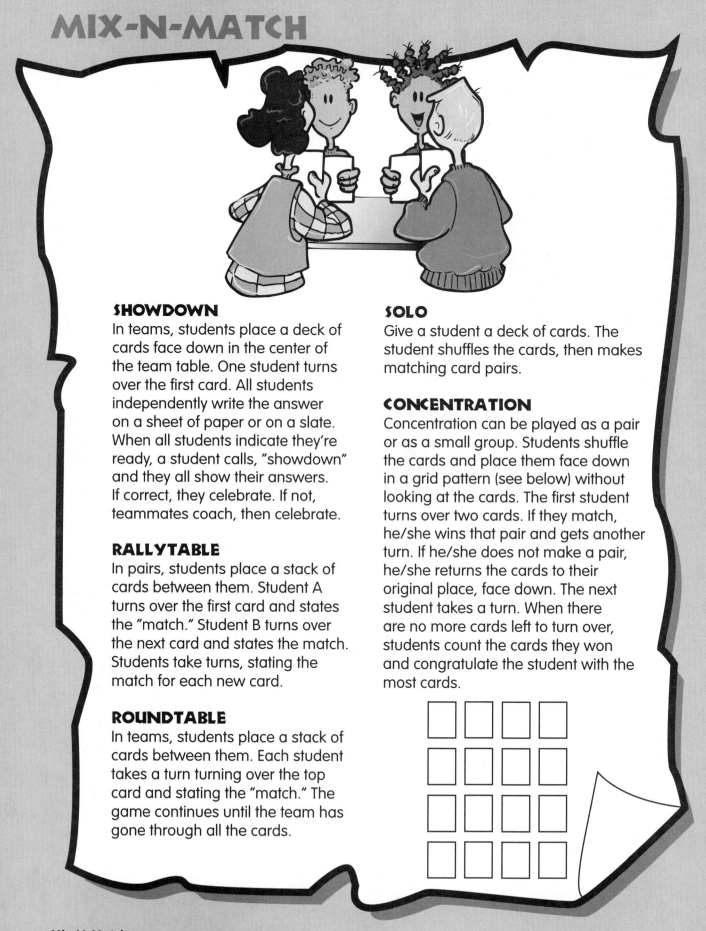

SHOWDOWN

In teams, students place a deck of cards face down in the center of the team table. One student turns over the first card. All students independently write the answer on a sheet of paper or on a slate. When all students indicate they're ready, a student calls, "showdown" and they all show their answers. If correct, they celebrate. If not, teammates coach, then celebrate.

RALLYTABLE

In pairs, students place a stack of cards between them. Student A turns over the first card and states the "match." Student B turns over the next card and states the match. Students take turns, stating the match for each new card.

ROUNDTABLE

In teams, students place a stack of cards between them. Each student takes a turn turning over the top card and stating the "match." The game continues until the team has gone through all the cards.

SOLO

Give a student a deck of cards. The student shuffles the cards, then makes matching card pairs.

CONCENTRATION

Concentration can be played as a pair or as a small group. Students shuffle the cards and place them face down in a grid pattern (see below) without looking at the cards. The first student turns over two cards. If they match, he/she wins that pair and gets another turn. If he/she does not make a pair, he/she returns the cards to their original place, face down. The next student takes a turn. When there are no more cards left to turn over, students count the cards they won and congratulate the student with the most cards.

LET'S PLAY!

Addition

Students practice addition by matching addition problems with their correct answers.

Quizzing Questions

▶ **A Cards: Addition Problems**
  • What is my sum?
▶ **B Cards: Answers**
  • What two numbers add up to me?

Addition

Mix-N-Match: Primary
Kagan Publishing • 1 (800) 933-2667 • www.KaganOnline.com

Addition

Solve the addition problems.

1 6 + 8 = _____

2 1 + 1 = _____

3 3 + 15 = _____

4 13 + 7 = _____

5 8 + 7 = _____

6 3 + 3 = _____

7 5 + 14 = _____

8 4 + 3 = _____

9 9 + 8 = _____

10 4 + 5 = _____

11 2 + 2 = _____

12 12 + 4 = _____

13 8 + 2 = _____

14 1 + 0 = _____

15 7 + 4 = _____

16 2 + 1 = _____

17 6 + 6 = _____

18 2 + 3 = _____

19 10 + 3 = _____

20 6 + 2 = _____

Mix-N-Match: Primary
Kagan Publishing • 1 (800) 933-2667 • www.KaganOnline.com

Addition

Solve the addition problems.

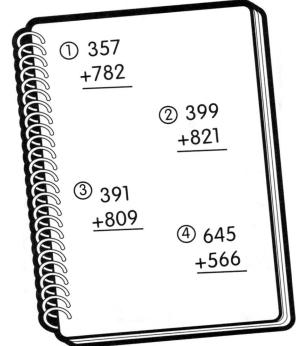

① 357
+782

② 399
+821

③ 391
+809

④ 645
+566

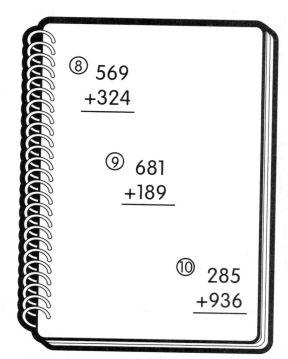

⑧ 569
+324

⑨ 681
+189

⑩ 285
+936

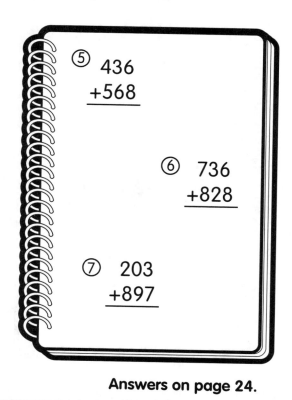

⑤ 436
+568

⑥ 736
+828

⑦ 203
+897

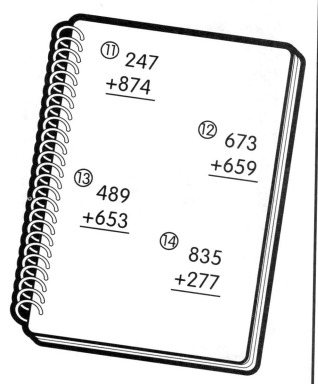

⑪ 247
+874

⑫ 673
+659

⑬ 489
+653

⑭ 835
+277

Answers on page 24.

Addition

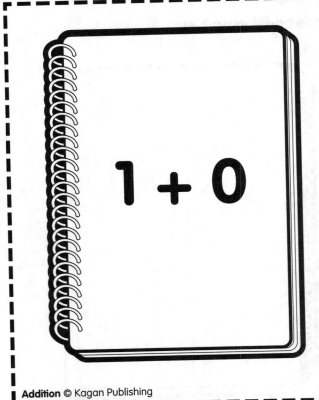

1 + 0

Addition © Kagan Publishing

1 + 1

Addition © Kagan Publishing

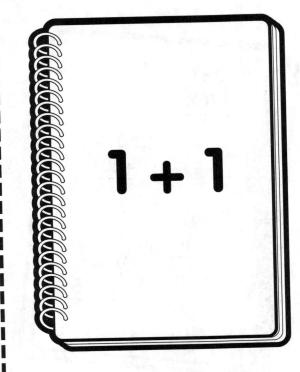

2 + 1

Addition © Kagan Publishing

2 + 2

Addition © Kagan Publishing

Mix-N-Match: Primary
Kagan Publishing • 1 (800) 933-2667 • www.KaganOnline.com

Addition

Addition © Kagan Publishing

Addition © Kagan Publishing

Addition © Kagan Publishing

Addition © Kagan Publishing

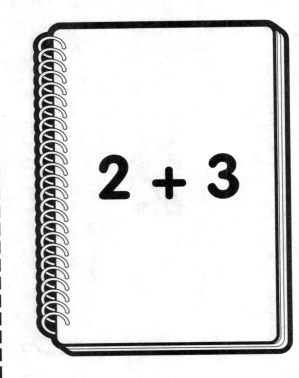

2 + 3

Addition © Kagan Publishing

3 + 3

Addition © Kagan Publishing

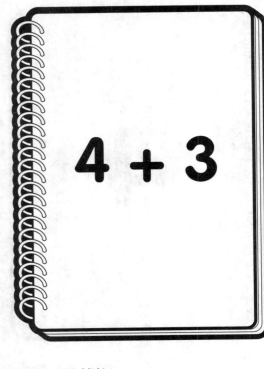

4 + 3

Addition © Kagan Publishing

6 + 2

Addition © Kagan Publishing

Mix-N-Match: Primary
Kagan Publishing • 1 (800) 933-2667 • www.KaganOnline.com

Addition

Addition © Kagan Publishing

Addition © Kagan Publishing

Addition © Kagan Publishing

Addition © Kagan Publishing

R. J. LONGSTREET MEDIA CENTER

Addition

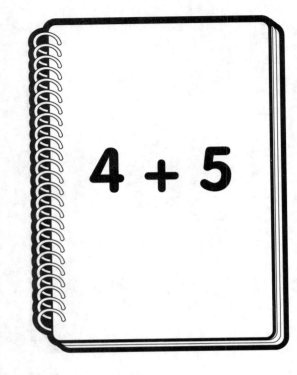

4 + 5

8 + 2

Addition © Kagan Publishing

Addition © Kagan Publishing

7 + 4

6 + 6

Addition © Kagan Publishing

Addition © Kagan Publishing

Addition

Addition © Kagan Publishing

Addition © Kagan Publishing

Addition © Kagan Publishing

Addition © Kagan Publishing

Addition

10 + 3

Addition © Kagan Publishing

6 + 8

Addition © Kagan Publishing

8 + 7

Addition © Kagan Publishing

12 + 4

Addition © Kagan Publishing

Mix-N-Match: Primary
Kagan Publishing • 1 (800) 933-2667 • www.KaganOnline.com

Addition

13

Addition © Kagan Publishing

14

Addition © Kagan Publishing

15

Addition © Kagan Publishing

16

Addition © Kagan Publishing

Addition

9 + 8

Addition © Kagan Publishing

3 + 15

Addition © Kagan Publishing

5 + 14

Addition © Kagan Publishing

13 + 7

Addition © Kagan Publishing

Mix-N-Match: Primary
Kagan Publishing • 1 (800) 933-2667 • www.KaganOnline.com

Addition © Kagan Publishing

Addition © Kagan Publishing

Addition © Kagan Publishing

Addition © Kagan Publishing

Addition Answers

1. 1 + 0 = 1
2. 1 + 1 = 2
3. 2 + 1 = 3
4. 2 + 2 = 4
5. 2 + 3 = 5
6. 3 + 3 = 6
7. 4 + 3 = 7
8. 6 + 2 = 8
9. 4 + 5 = 9
10. 8 + 2 = 10

11. 7 + 4 = 11
12. 6 + 6 = 12
13. 10 + 3 = 13
14. 6 + 8 = 14
15. 8 + 7 = 15
16. 12 + 4 = 16
17. 9 + 8 = 17
18. 3 + 15 = 18
19. 5 + 14 = 19
20. 13 + 7 = 20

Page 13 Answers
1. 357 + 782 = 1,139
2. 399 + 821 = 1,220
3. 391 + 809 = 1,200
4. 645 + 566 = 1,211
5. 436 + 568 = 1,004
6. 736 + 828 = 1,564
7. 203 + 897 = 1,100
8. 569 + 324 = 893
9. 681 + 189 = 870
10. 285 + 936 = 1,221
11. 247 + 874 = 1,121
12. 673 + 659 = 1,332
13. 489 + 653 = 1,142
14. 835 + 277 = 1,112

Mix-N-Match: Primary
Kagan Publishing • 1 (800) 933-2667 • www.KaganOnline.com

Animals

Students learn animal names by matching the picture of the animal with its name.

Quizzing Questions

▶ **A Cards: Pictures of Animals**
- What animal am I?
- Where do I live?

▶ **B Cards: Animal Names**
- What do I look like?
- Am I a mammal, bird, reptile, or fish?

Animals

Write the name of the animal pictured.

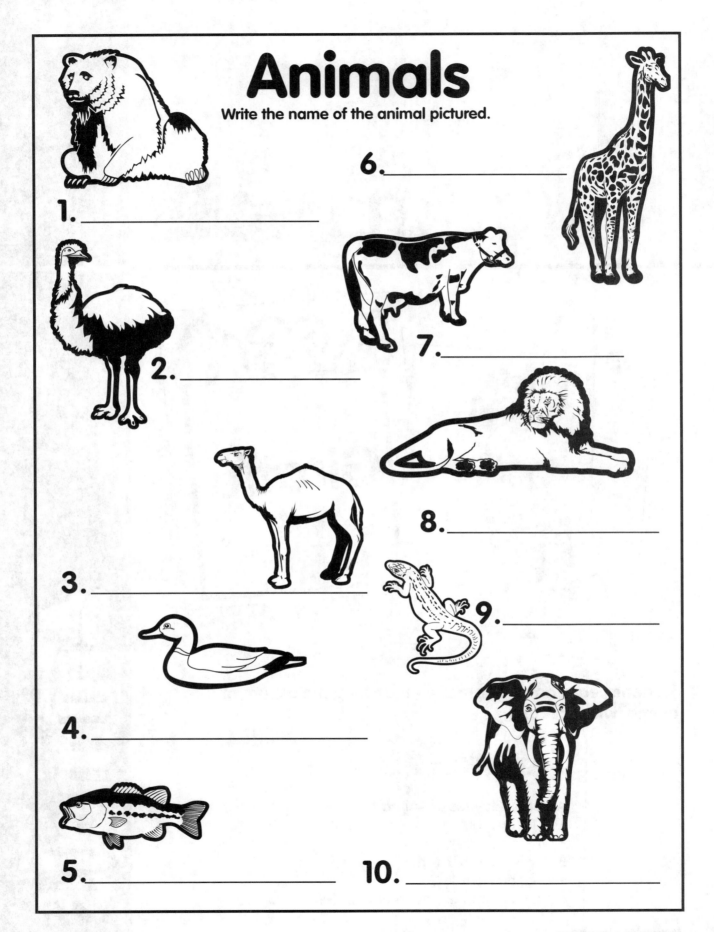

1._____

2._____

3._____

4._____

5._____

6._____

7._____

8._____

9._____

10._____

Mix-N-Match: Primary
Kagan Publishing • 1 (800) 933-2667 • www.KaganOnline.com

Animals

Write the name of the animal pictured.

1. _____

2. _____

3. _____

4. _____

5. _____

6. _____

7. _____

8. _____

9. _____

10. _____

Animals

Animals © Kagan Publishing

Animals © Kagan Publishing

Animals © Kagan Publishing

Animals © Kagan Publishing

Mix-N-Match: Primary
Kagan Publishing • 1 (800) 933-2667 • www.KaganOnline.com

Animals

Bear

Animals © Kagan Publishing

Camel

Animals © Kagan Publishing

Cow

Animals © Kagan Publishing

Duck

Animals © Kagan Publishing

Animals

Animals © Kagan Publishing

Animals © Kagan Publishing

Animals © Kagan Publishing

Animals © Kagan Publishing

Mix-N-Match: Primary
Kagan Publishing • 1 (800) 933-2667 • www.KaganOnline.com

Elephant

Animals © Kagan Publishing

Fish

Animals © Kagan Publishing

Giraffe

Animals © Kagan Publishing

Lion

Animals © Kagan Publishing

Animals

Animals © Kagan Publishing

Animals © Kagan Publishing

Animals © Kagan Publishing

Animals © Kagan Publishing

Mix-N-Match: Primary
Kagan Publishing • 1 (800) 933-2667 • www.KaganOnline.com

Lizard

Animals © Kagan Publishing

Ostrich

Animals © Kagan Publishing

Parrot

Animals © Kagan Publishing

Pig

Animals © Kagan Publishing

Animals

Animals © Kagan Publishing

Animals © Kagan Publishing

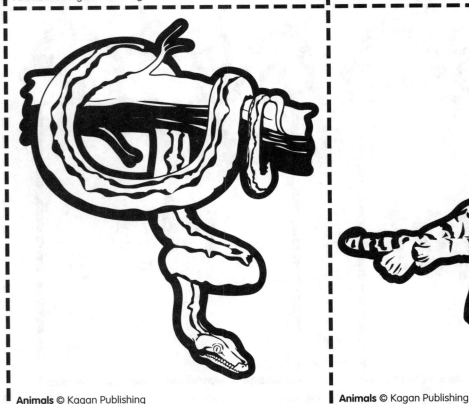

Animals © Kagan Publishing

Animals © Kagan Publishing

Porcupine

Animals © Kagan Publishing

Rat

Animals © Kagan Publishing

Snake

Animals © Kagan Publishing

Tiger

Animals © Kagan Publishing

Animals

Animals © Kagan Publishing

Animals © Kagan Publishing

Animals © Kagan Publishing

Animals © Kagan Publishing

Mix-N-Match: **Primary**
Kagan Publishing • 1 (800) 933-2667 • www.KaganOnline.com

Animals

Tortoise

Animals © Kagan Publishing

Turkey

Animals © Kagan Publishing

Whale

Animals © Kagan Publishing

Zebra

Animals © Kagan Publishing

Animals

1. Bear

6. Fish

11. Parrot

16. Tiger

2. Camel

7. Giraffe

12. Pig

17. Tortoise

3. Cow

8. Lion

13. Porcupine

18. Turkey

4. Duck

9. Lizard

14. Rat

19. Whale

5. Elephant

10. Ostrich

15. Snake

20. Zebra

Mix-N-Match: Primary
Kagan Publishing • 1 (800) 933-2667 • www.KaganOnline.com

Beginning Consonants and Vowels

Students practice beginning consonants and vowels by matching the word with the correct letter.

Quizzing Questions

▶ **A Cards: Animal Pictures and Names**
  • What letter do I begin with?
▶ **B Cards: Letters**
  • What is an animal that begins with this letter?
  • What is a word that begins with this letter?

Mix-N-Match: Primary
Kagan Publishing • 1 (800) 933-2667 • www.KaganOnline.com

Beginning
Consonants & Vowels
What letter do I begin with? Write the letter in the blank.

1. _____

2. _____

3. _____

4. _____

5. _____

6. _____

Mix-N-Match: Primary
Kagan Publishing • 1 (800) 933-2667 • www.KaganOnline.com

Beginning
Consonants & Vowels

What letter do I begin with? Write the letter in the blank.

1 _____
_____
_____

2 _____
_____
_____

3 _____
_____
_____

4 _____
_____

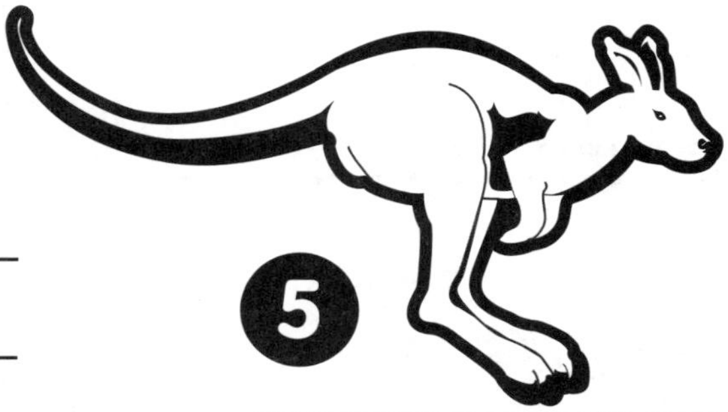

5 _____
_____
_____

6 _____
_____

Beginning Consonants & Vowels

Ant

Bird

Beginning Consonants & Vowels © Kagan Publishing

Beginning Consonants & Vowels © Kagan Publishing

Cat

Dog

Beginning Consonants & Vowels © Kagan Publishing

Beginning Consonants & Vowels © Kagan Publishing

Mix-N-Match: Primary
Kagan Publishing • 1 (800) 933-2667 • www.KaganOnline.com

Beginning Consonants & Vowels

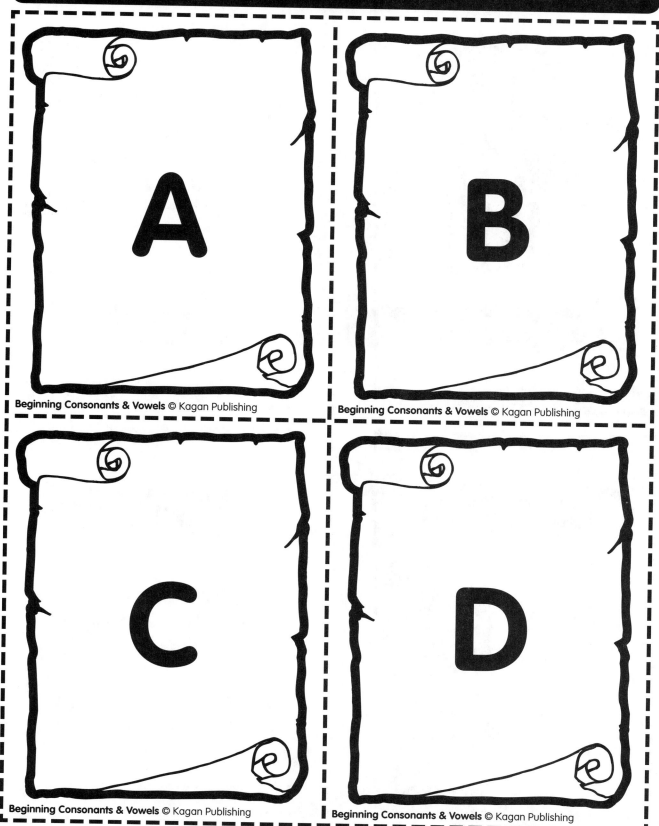

A

Beginning Consonants & Vowels © Kagan Publishing

B

Beginning Consonants & Vowels © Kagan Publishing

C

Beginning Consonants & Vowels © Kagan Publishing

D

Beginning Consonants & Vowels © Kagan Publishing

Elephant

Beginning Consonants & Vowels © Kagan Publishing

Fox

Beginning Consonants & Vowels © Kagan Publishing

Giraffe

Horse

Beginning Consonants & Vowels © Kagan Publishing

Beginning Consonants & Vowels © Kagan Publishing

E

Beginning Consonants & Vowels © Kagan Publishing

F

Beginning Consonants & Vowels © Kagan Publishing

G

Beginning Consonants & Vowels © Kagan Publishing

H

Beginning Consonants & Vowels © Kagan Publishing

Beginning Consonants & Vowels

Iguana

Kangaroo

Beginning **Consonants & Vowels** © *Kagan Publishing*

Beginning **Consonants & Vowels** © *Kagan Publishing*

Lamb

Mouse

Beginning **Consonants & Vowels** © *Kagan Publishing*

Beginning **Consonants & Vowels** © *Kagan Publishing*

Mix-N-Match: Primary
Kagan Publishing • 1 (800) 933-2667 • www.KaganOnline.com

Beginning Consonants & Vowels

Beginning Consonants & Vowels © Kagan Publishing

Beginning Consonants & Vowels © Kagan Publishing

Beginning Consonants & Vowels © Kagan Publishing

Beginning Consonants & Vowels © Kagan Publishing

Newt

Beginning Consonants & Vowels © Kagan Publishing

Owl

Beginning Consonants & Vowels © Kagan Publishing

Penguin

Beginning Consonants & Vowels © Kagan Publishing

Quail

Beginning Consonants & Vowels © Kagan Publishing

Beginning Consonants & Vowels © Kagan Publishing

Beginning Consonants & Vowels © Kagan Publishing

Beginning Consonants & Vowels © Kagan Publishing

Beginning Consonants & Vowels © Kagan Publishing

Beginning Consonants & Vowels

Rat

Snake

Tortoise

Wasp

Beginning Consonants & Vowels

Beginning Consonants & Vowels © Kagan Publishing

Beginning Consonants & Vowels © Kagan Publishing

Beginning Consonants & Vowels © Kagan Publishing

Beginning Consonants & Vowels © Kagan Publishing

Beginning Consonants & Vowels Answers

Ant **B**ird **C**at **D**og

Elephant **F**ox **G**iraffe **H**orse

Iguana **K**angaroo **L**amb **M**ouse

Newt **O**wl **P**enguin **Q**uail

Rat **S**nake **T**ortoise **W**asp

Mix-N-Match: Primary
Kagan Publishing • 1 (800) 933-2667 • www.KaganOnline.com

Community Helpers

Students learn about community helpers by matching the helpers with what they do.

Quizzing Questions

▶ **A Cards: Community Helpers**
  • What do I do?
  • Where do I work?

▶ **B Cards: Job Descriptions**
  • Which community helper does this job?

Mix-N-Match: Primary
Kagan Publishing • 1 (800) 933-2667 • www.KaganOnline.com

Community Helpers

Community Helpers

Draw lines connecting the community helpers with what they do.

1. Automotive Technician	I help doctors take care of you.
2. Chef	I diagnose and repair your car.
3. Computer Programmer	I fight fires.
4. Butcher	I will represent you when in a court of law.
5. Contractor	I am your college teacher.
6. Dentist	I write the code for computer programs.
7. Doctor	I arrange and sell flowers.
8. Farmer	I cut the meat you eat.
9. Firefighter	I take care of you when you're ill.
10. Florist	I prepare the food you eat.
11. Gardener	I take your order and serve you food at restaurants.
12. Journalist	I direct construction projects.
13. Lawyer	I write for a newspaper or magazine.
14. Mail Carrier	I clean your teeth and fill your cavities.
15. Nurse	I teach you in school.
16. Police Officer	I grow the food you eat.
17. Professor	I maintain lawns and gardens around town.
18. Salesperson	I deliver your mail.
19. Server	I keep the streets safe.
20. Teacher	I sell you the things you want and need.

Mix-N-Match: Primary
Kagan Publishing • 1 (800) 933-2667 • www.KaganOnline.com

Community Helpers

Select one community helper and write his or her occupation in the box below.
Draw three pictures relating to that helper.

_____

Community Helper

Draw a picture of what I look like.

Draw a picture of where I work.

Draw a picture of what I do.

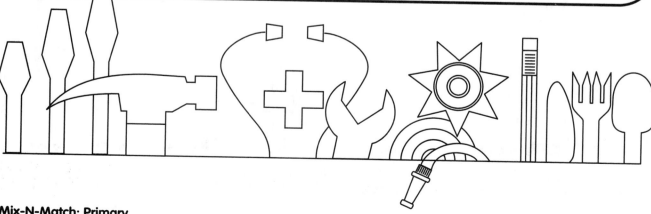

Community Helpers

Automotive Technician

Community Helpers © Kagan Publishing

Chef

Community Helpers © Kagan Publishing

Computer Programmer

Community Helpers © Kagan Publishing

Butcher

Community Helpers © Kagan Publishing

Mix-N-Match: Primary
Kagan Publishing • 1 (800) 933-2667 • www.KaganOnline.com

Community Helpers

Community

I diagnose and repair your car.

Community Helpers © Kagan Publishing

Community

I prepare the food you eat.

Community Helpers © Kagan Publishing

Community

I write the code for computer programs.

Community Helpers © Kagan Publishing

Community

I cut the meat you eat.

Community Helpers © Kagan Publishing

Community Helpers

Community

Contractor

Community Helpers © Kagan Publishing

Community

Dentist

Community Helpers © Kagan Publishing

Community

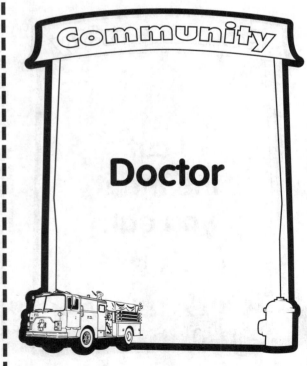

Doctor

Community Helpers © Kagan Publishing

Community

Farmer

Community Helpers © Kagan Publishing

Mix-N-Match: Primary
Kagan Publishing • 1 (800) 933-2667 • www.KaganOnline.com

Community Helpers

Community

I direct
construction
projects.

Community Helpers © Kagan Publishing

Community

I clean your
teeth and fill
your cavities.

Community Helpers © Kagan Publishing

Community

I take care
of you when
you're ill.

Community Helpers © Kagan Publishing

Community

I grow
the food
you eat.

Community Helpers © Kagan Publishing

Community Helpers

Community

Firefighter

Community Helpers © Kagan Publishing

Community

Florist

Community Helpers © Kagan Publishing

Community

Gardener

Community Helpers © Kagan Publishing

Community

Journalist

Community Helpers © Kagan Publishing

Mix-N-Match: Primary
Kagan Publishing • 1 (800) 933-2667 • www.KaganOnline.com

Community Helpers

I fight
fires.

Community Helpers © Kagan Publishing

I arrange
and sell
flowers.

Community Helpers © Kagan Publishing

I maintain
lawns and
gardens
around town.

Community Helpers © Kagan Publishing

I write for a
newspaper
or magazine.

Community Helpers © Kagan Publishing

Community Helpers

Community

Lawyer

Community Helpers © Kagan Publishing

Community

**Mail
Carrier**

Community Helpers © Kagan Publishing

Community

Nurse

Community Helpers © Kagan Publishing

Community

**Police
Officer**

Community Helpers © Kagan Publishing

Community Helpers

Community

I will represent you when in a court of law.

Community Helpers © Kagan Publishing

Community

I deliver your mail.

Community Helpers © Kagan Publishing

Community

I help doctors take care of you.

Community Helpers © Kagan Publishing

Community

I keep the streets safe.

Community Helpers © Kagan Publishing

Community Helpers

Professor

Community Helpers © Kagan Publishing

Salesperson

Community Helpers © Kagan Publishing

Server

Community Helpers © Kagan Publishing

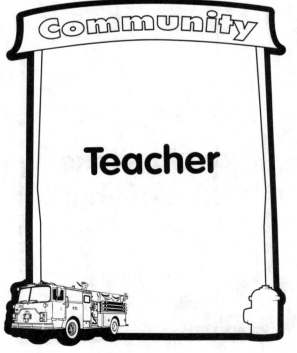

Teacher

Community Helpers © Kagan Publishing

Mix-N-Match: Primary
Kagan Publishing • 1 (800) 933-2667 • www.KaganOnline.com

Community Helpers

Community

I am your college teacher.

Community Helpers © Kagan Publishing

Community

I sell you the things you want and need.

Community Helpers © Kagan Publishing

Community

I take your order and serve you food at restaurants.

Community Helpers © Kagan Publishing

Community

I teach you in school.

Community Helpers © Kagan Publishing

Community

Community Helpers

1. **Automotive Technician** - I diagnose and repair your car.

2. **Chef** - I prepare the food you eat.

3. **Computer Programmer** - I write the code for computer programs.

4. **Butcher** - I cut the meat you eat.

5. **Contractor** - I direct construction projects.

6. **Dentist** - I clean your teeth and fill your cavities.

7. **Doctor** - I take care of you when you're ill.

8. **Farmer** - I grow the food you eat.

9. **Firefighter** - I fight fires.

10. **Florist** - I arrange and sell flowers.

11. **Gardener** - I maintain lawns and gardens around town.

12. **Journalist** - I write for a newspaper or magazine.

13. **Lawyer** - I will represent you when in a court of law.

14. **Mail Carrier** - I deliver your mail.

15. **Nurse** - I help doctors take care of you.

16. **Police Officer** - I keep the streets safe.

17. **Professor** - I am your college teacher.

18. **Salesperson** - I sell you the things you want and need.

19. **Server** - I take your order and serve you food at restaurants.

20. **Teacher** - I teach you in school.

Mix-N-Match: Primary
Kagan Publishing • 1 (800) 933-2667 • www.KaganOnline.com

Food

Students learn about food by matching the pictures of food to the name.

Quizzing Questions

▶ **A Cards: Food Pictures**
- What food am I?
- What do I taste like?

▶ **B Cards: Food Names**
- What do I look like?
- What food group do I belong to?

Food

Write the name of the food pictured.

1. _____

2. _____

3. _____

4. _____

5. _____

6. _____

7. _____

8. _____

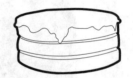

9. _____

10. _____

11. _____

12. _____

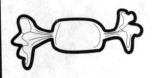

13. _____

14. _____

15. _____

16. _____

17. _____

18. _____

19. _____

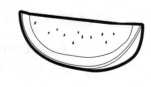

20. _____

Mix-N-Match: Primary

Kagan Publishing • 1 (800) 933-2667 • www.KaganOnline.com

Food

Draw a picture of the food on the plate.

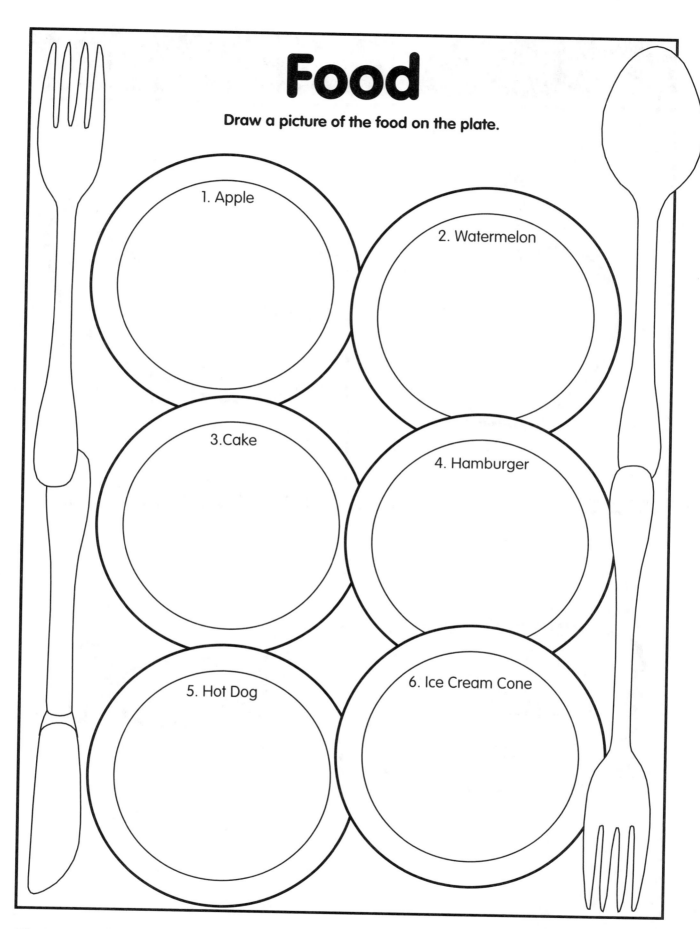

1. Apple

2. Watermelon

3. Cake

4. Hamburger

5. Hot Dog

6. Ice Cream Cone

Food

Food © Kagan Publishing

Food © Kagan Publishing

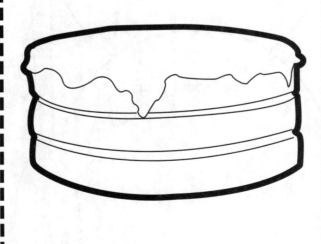

Food © Kagan Publishing

Food © Kagan Publishing

Mix-N-Match: Primary
Kagan Publishing • 1 (800) 933-2667 • www.KaganOnline.com

Apple

Food © Kagan Publishing

Banana

Food © Kagan Publishing

Cake

Food © Kagan Publishing

Candy

Food © Kagan Publishing

Food

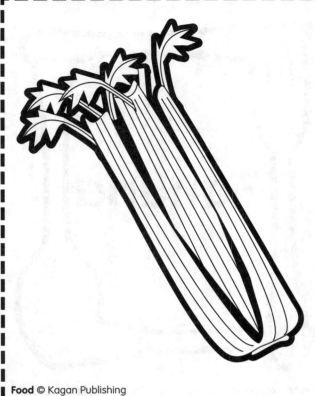

Food © Kagan Publishing

Food © Kagan Publishing

Food © Kagan Publishing

Food © Kagan Publishing

Food

Celery

Corn

Donuts

Grapes

Food © Kagan Publishing

Food © Kagan Publishing

Food © Kagan Publishing

Food © Kagan Publishing

Food

Food © Kagan Publishing

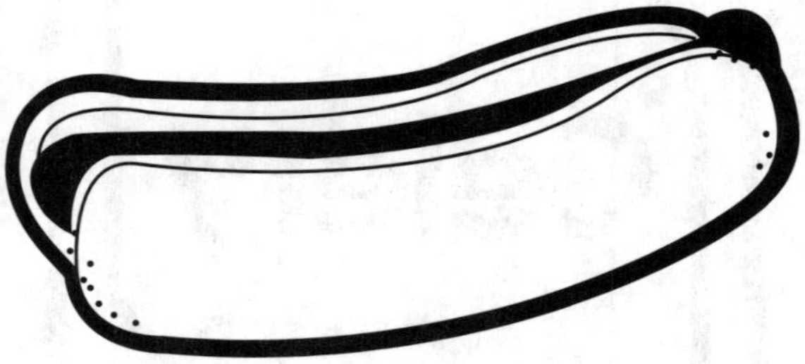

Food © Kagan Publishing

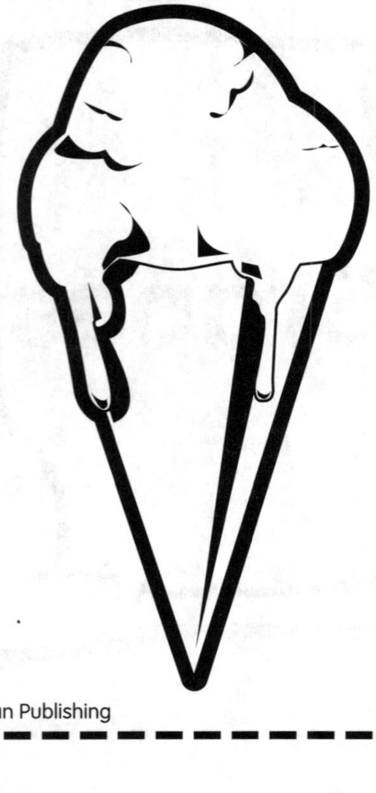

Food © Kagan Publishing

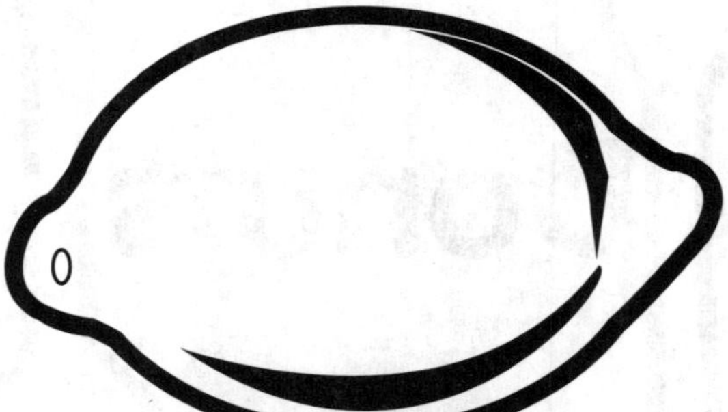

Food © Kagan Publishing

Hamburger

Food © Kagan Publishing

Hot Dog

Food © Kagan Publishing

Ice Cream Cone

Food © Kagan Publishing

Lemon

Food © Kagan Publishing

Food

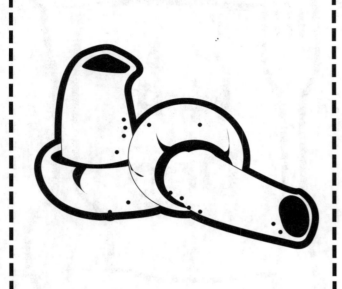

Food © Kagan Publishing

Food © Kagan Publishing

Food © Kagan Publishing

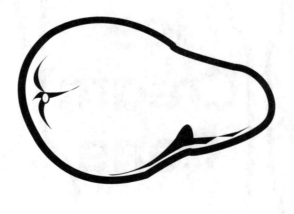

Food © Kagan Publishing

Mushrooms

Food © Kagan Publishing

Onion

Food © Kagan Publishing

Pancakes & Syrup

Food © Kagan Publishing

Pear

Food © Kagan Publishing

Food

Food © Kagan Publishing

Food © Kagan Publishing

Food © Kagan Publishing

Food © Kagan Publishing

Mix-N-Match: Primary
Kagan Publishing • 1 (800) 933-2667 • www.KaganOnline.com

Food

Pie

Food © Kagan Publishing

Radishes

Food © Kagan Publishing

Tomato

Food © Kagan Publishing

Watermelon

Food © Kagan Publishing

Food

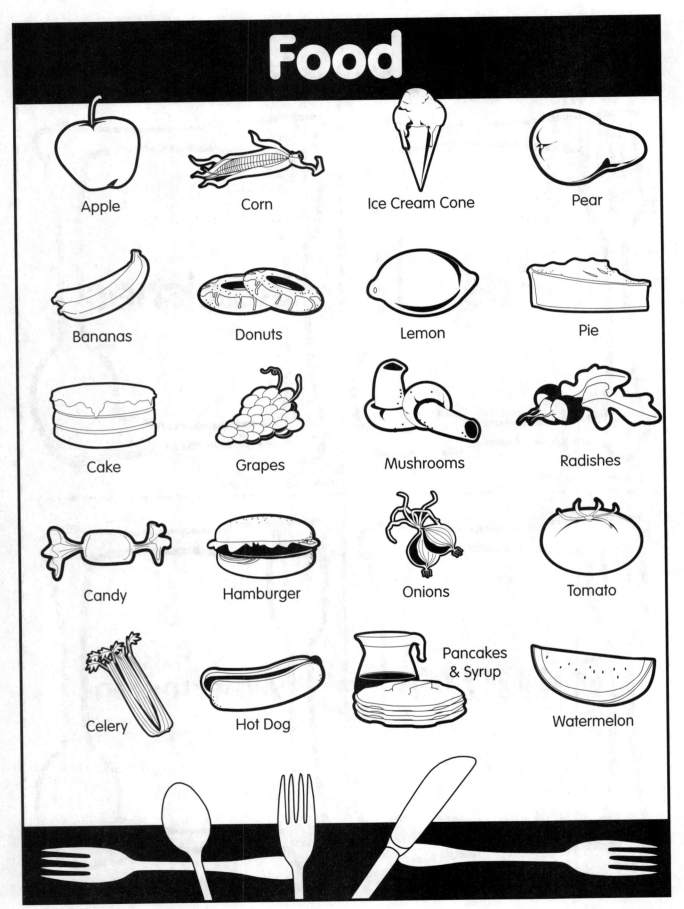

Apple

Corn

Ice Cream Cone

Pear

Bananas

Donuts

Lemon

Pie

Cake

Grapes

Mushrooms

Radishes

Candy

Hamburger

Onions

Tomato

Celery

Hot Dog

Pancakes & Syrup

Watermelon

Mix-N-Match: Primary
Kagan Publishing • 1 (800) 933-2667 • www.KaganOnline.com

Less Than, Greater Than

Students practice less than and greater than by matching the problem card with the correct symbol card.

Quizzing Questions

▶ **A Cards: Less Than, Greater Than Problems**
  • Is the number on the left less than or greater than the number on the right?
▶ **B Cards: Less Than, Greater Than Symbols**
  • What is less than (any number)?
  • What is greater than (any number)?

Mix-N-Match: Primary
Kagan Publishing • 1 (800) 933-2667 • www.KaganOnline.com

Less Than, Greater Than

Fill in the blank using the less than < or greater than > symbols.

1. 1 __ 10

2. 7 __ 6

3. 7 __ 9

4. 8 __ 7

5. 2 __ 6

6. 1 __ 0

7. 4 __ 3

8. 3 __ 5

9. 9 __ 5

10. 1 __ 4

11. 2 __ 1

12. 2 __ 3

13. 0 __ 1

14. 10 __ 3

15. 5 __ 7

16. 6 __ 4

17. 6 __ 8

18. 5 __ 1

19. 3 __ 2

20. 1 __ 2

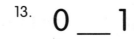

Mix-N-Match: Primary

Kagan Publishing • 1 (800) 933-2667 • www.KaganOnline.com

Less Than, Greater Than

Write a number in the blank that is greater than
or less than the number shown.

___ > 6

5 < ___

1 < ___

___ > 7

___ < 0

10 > ___

9 > ___

___ < 7

___ < 3

4 > ___

Less Than, Greater Than

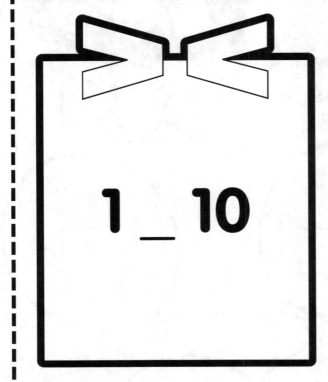

1 _ 10

7 _ 6

Less Than, Greater Than © Kagan Publishing

Less Than, Greater Than © Kagan Publishing

7 _ 9

8 _ 7

Less Than, Greater Than © Kagan Publishing

Less Than, Greater Than © Kagan Publishing

Mix-N-Match: Primary
Kagan Publishing • 1 (800) 933-2667 • www.KaganOnline.com

Less Than, Greater Than © Kagan Publishing

> greater than

Less Than, Greater Than © Kagan Publishing

Less Than, Greater Than © Kagan Publishing

> greater than

Less Than, Greater Than © Kagan Publishing

Less Than, Greater Than

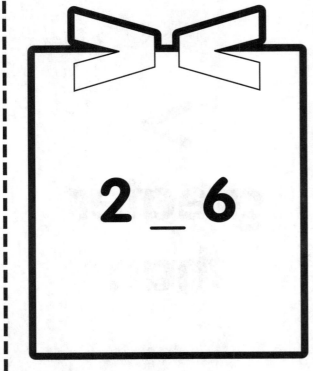

2 _ 6

Less Than, Greater Than © Kagan Publishing

1 _ 0

Less Than, Greater Than © Kagan Publishing

4 _ 3

Less Than, Greater Than © Kagan Publishing .

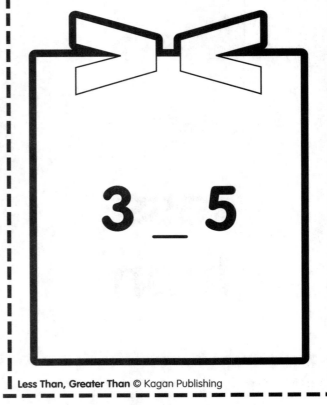

3 _ 5

Less Than, Greater Than © Kagan Publishing

Mix-N-Match: Primary
Kagan Publishing • 1 (800) 933-2667 • www.KaganOnline.com

Less Than, Greater Than

<

less than

Less Than, Greater Than © Kagan Publishing

>

greater than

Less Than, Greater Than © Kagan Publishing

>

greater than

Less Than, Greater Than © Kagan Publishing

<

less than

Less Than, Greater Than © Kagan Publishing

Less Than, Greater Than

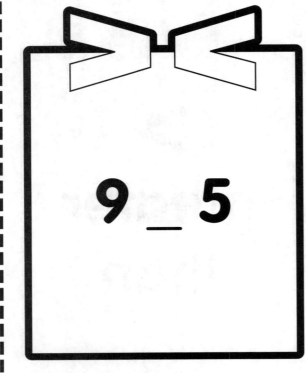

9 _ 5

Less Than, Greater Than © Kagan Publishing

1 _ 4

Less Than, Greater Than © Kagan Publishing

2 _ 1

Less Than, Greater Than © Kagan Publishing

2 _ 3

Less Than, Greater Than © Kagan Publishing

Mix-N-Match: Primary
Kagan Publishing • 1 (800) 933-2667 • www.KaganOnline.com

Less Than, Greater Than

>

greater than

Less Than, Greater Than © Kagan Publishing

<

less than

Less Than, Greater Than © Kagan Publishing

>

greater than

Less Than, Greater Than © Kagan Publishing

<

less than

Less Than, Greater Than © Kagan Publishing

Less Than, Greater Than

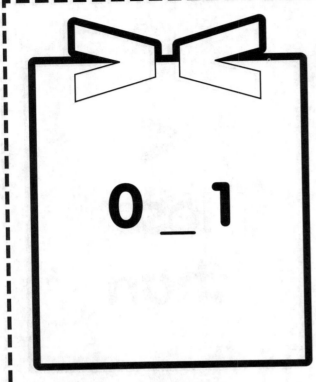

0 _ 1

10 _ 3

5 _ 7

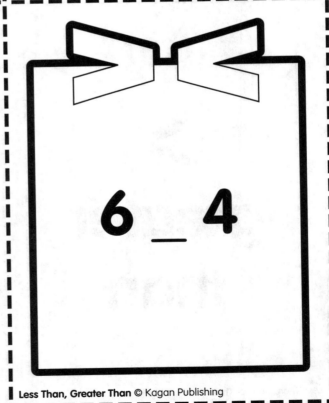

6 _ 4

Less Than, Greater Than © Kagan Publishing

Less Than, Greater Than © Kagan Publishing

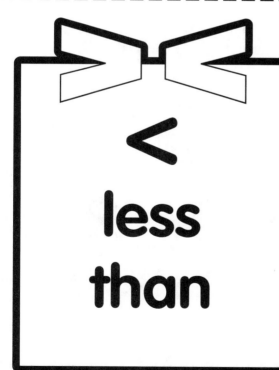

Less Than, Greater Than © Kagan Publishing

Less Than, Greater Than © Kagan Publishing

Less Than, Greater Than

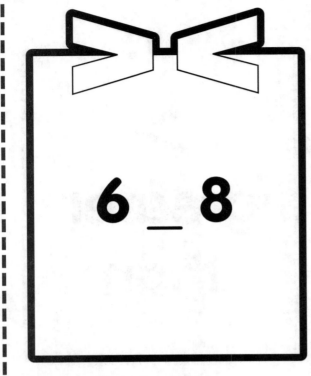

6 _ 8

Less Than, Greater Than © Kagan Publishing

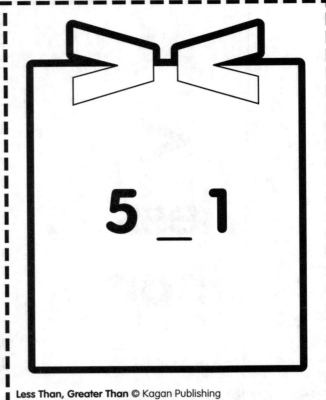

5 _ 1

Less Than, Greater Than © Kagan Publishing

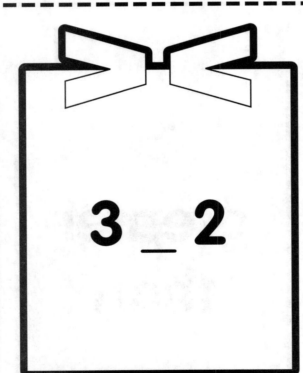

3 _ 2

Less Than, Greater Than © Kagan Publishing

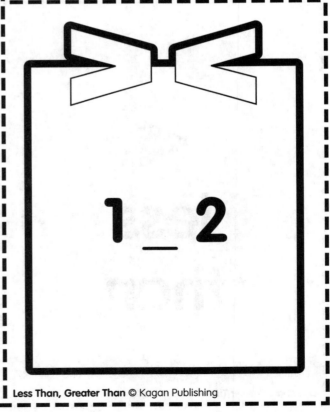

1 _ 2

Less Than, Greater Than © Kagan Publishing

Mix-N-Match: Primary
Kagan Publishing • 1 (800) 933-2667 • www.KaganOnline.com

Less Than, Greater Than

<
less
than

Less Than, Greater Than © Kagan Publishing

>
greater
than

Less Than, Greater Than © Kagan Publishing

>
greater
than

Less Than, Greater Than © Kagan Publishing

<
less
than

Less Than, Greater Than © Kagan Publishing

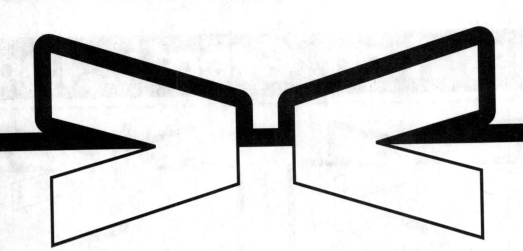

Less Than, Greater Than Answers

1. 1 __ 10 = < less than

2. 7 __ 6 = > greater than

3. 7 __ 9 = < less than

4. 8 __ 7 = > greater than

5. 2 __ 6 = < less than

6. 1 __ 0 = > greater than

7. 4 __ 3 = > greater than

8. 3 __ 5 = < less than

9. 9 __ 5 = > greater than

10. 1 __ 4 = < less than

11. 2 __ 1 = > greater than

12. 2 __ 3 = < less than

13. 0 __ 1 = < less than

14. 10 __ 3 = > greater than

15. 5 __ 7 = < less than

16. 6 __ 4 = > greater than

17. 6 __ 8 = < less than

18. 5 __ 1 = > greater than

19. 3 __ 2 = > greater than

20. 1 __ 2 = < less than

Mix-N-Match: Primary
Kagan Publishing • 1 (800) 933-2667 • www.KaganOnline.com

Letters

Students practice naming and recognizing letters by matching the capital letter with the lower case letter.

Quizzing Questions

▶ **A Cards: Upper Case Letters**
- What letter am I?
- What does my lower case letter look like?

▶ **B Cards: Lower Case Letterss**
- What letter am I?
- What does my upper case letter look like?

Mix-N-Match: Primary
Kagan Publishing • 1 (800) 933-2667 • www.KaganOnline.com

Lower Case Letters

Write the following letters in lower case.

A _____

B _____

C _____

D _____

E _____

F _____

G _____

H _____

I _____

J _____

K _____

L _____

M _____

N _____

O _____

P _____

Q _____

R _____

S _____

T _____

U _____

V _____

W _____

X _____

Y _____

Z _____

Mix-N-Match: Primary
Kagan Publishing • 1 (800) 933-2667 • www.KaganOnline.com

Upper Case Letters

Write the following letters in upper case.

i _____

a _____

b _____

c _____

d _____

e _____

f _____

g _____

h _____

j _____

k _____

l _____

m _____

n _____

o _____

p _____

q _____

r _____

s _____

t _____

u _____

v _____

w _____

x _____

y _____

z _____

Letters

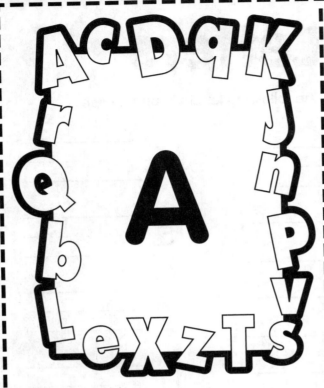

Letters © Kagan Publishing

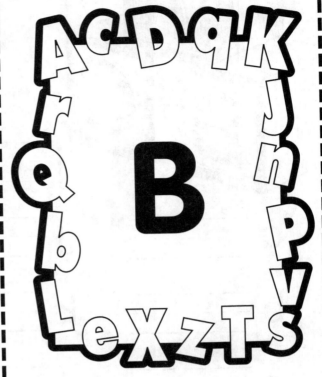

Letters © Kagan Publishing

Letters © Kagan Publishing

Letters © Kagan Publishing

Mix-N-Match: Primary

Kagan Publishing • 1 (800) 933-2667 • www.KaganOnline.com

Letters

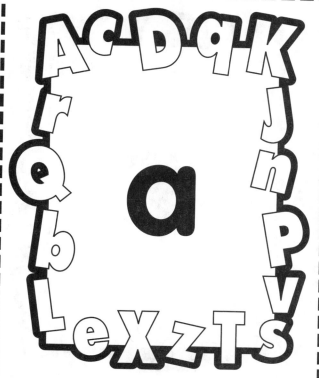

Letters © Kagan Publishing

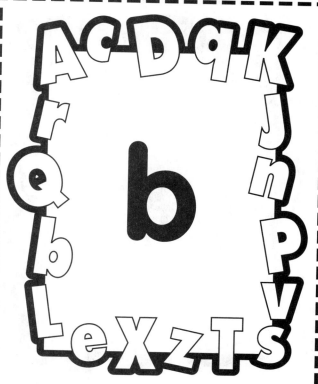

Letters © Kagan Publishing

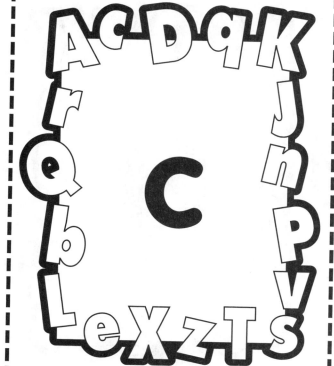

Letters © Kagan Publishing

Letters © Kagan Publishing

Letters

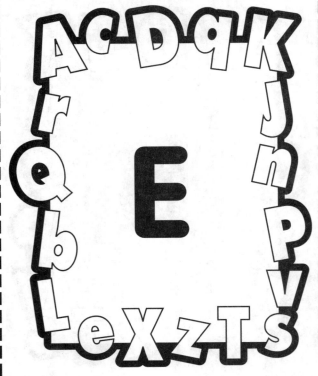

Letters © Kagan Publishing

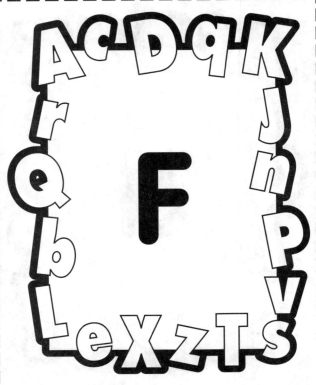

Letters © Kagan Publishing

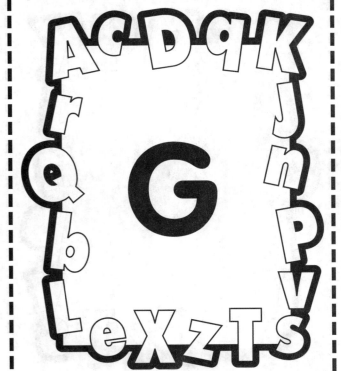

Letters © Kagan Publishing

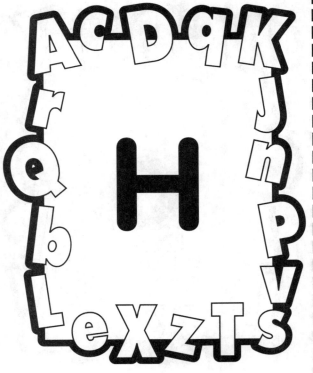

Letters © Kagan Publishing

Mix-N-Match: Primary
Kagan Publishing • 1 (800) 933-2667 • www.KaganOnline.com

Letters

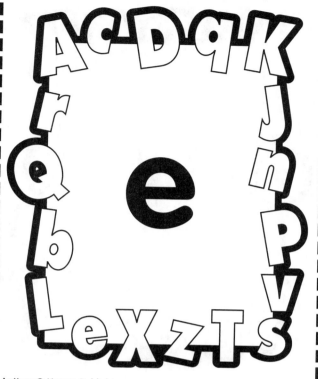

Letters © Kagan Publishing

Letters © Kagan Publishing

Letters © Kagan Publishing

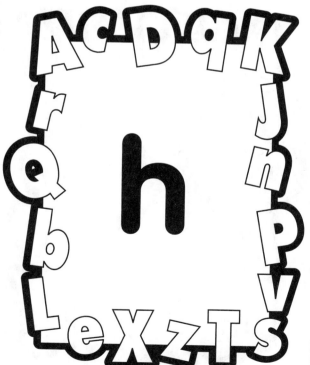

Letters © Kagan Publishing

Letters

Letters © Kagan Publishing

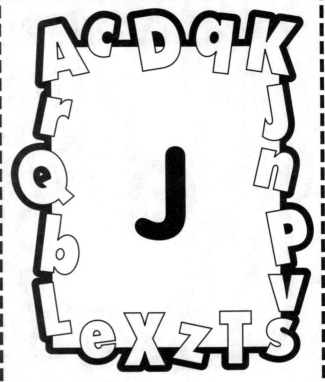

Letters © Kagan Publishing

Letters © Kagan Publishing

Letters © Kagan Publishing

Mix-N-Match: Primary
Kagan Publishing • 1 (800) 933-2667 • www.KaganOnline.com

Letters

Letters © Kagan Publishing

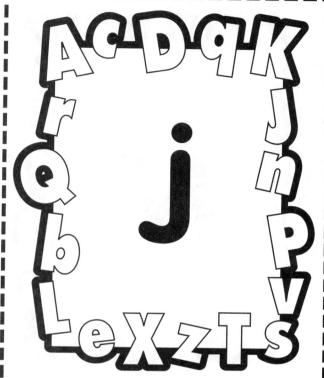

Letters © Kagan Publishing

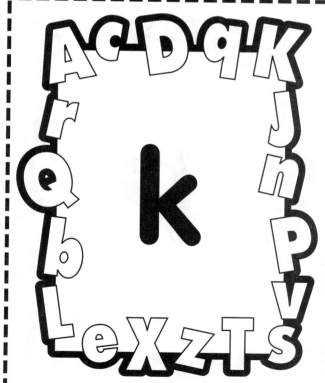

Letters © Kagan Publishing

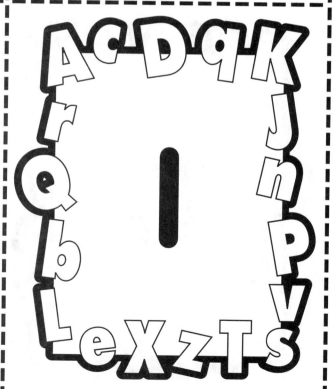

Letters © Kagan Publishing

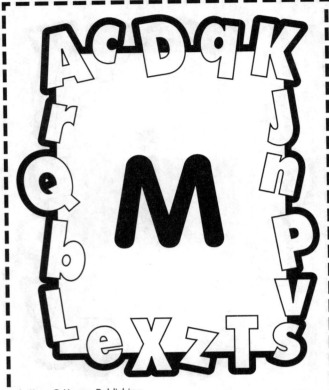

Letters © Kagan Publishing

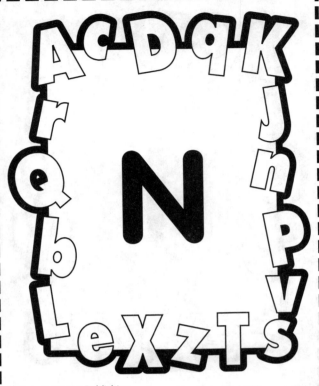

Letters © Kagan Publishing

Letters © Kagan Publishing

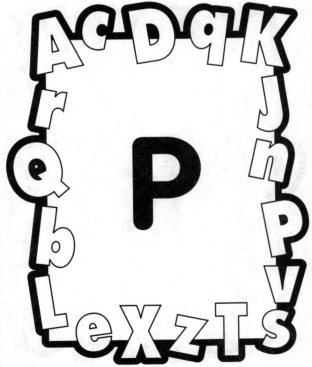

Letters © Kagan Publishing

Letters

Letters © Kagan Publishing

Letters © Kagan Publishing

Letters © Kagan Publishing

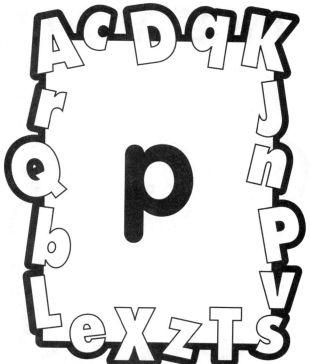

Letters © Kagan Publishing

Letters

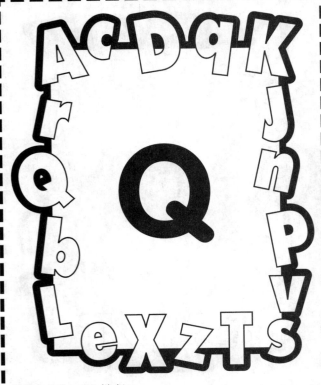

Letters © Kagan Publishing

Letters © Kagan Publishing

Letters © Kagan Publishing

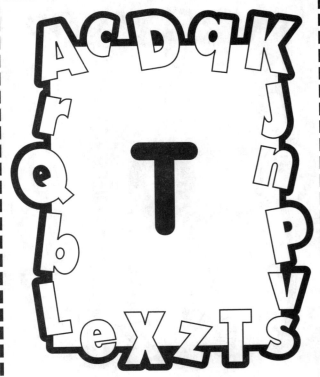

Letters © Kagan Publishing

Mix-N-Match: Primary
Kagan Publishing • 1 (800) 933-2667 • www.KaganOnline.com

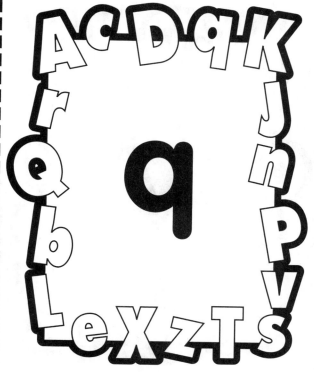

Letters © Kagan Publishing

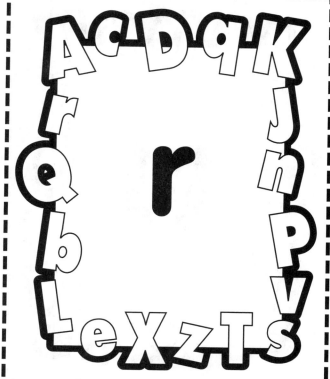

Letters © Kagan Publishing

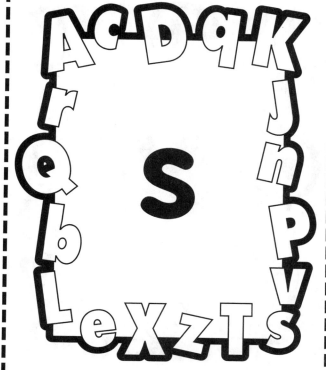

Letters © Kagan Publishing

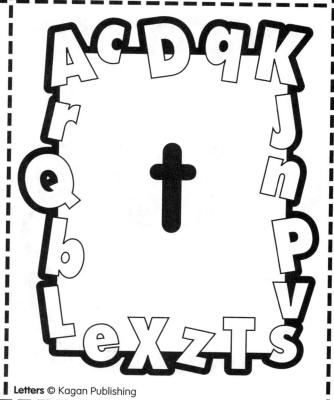

Letters © Kagan Publishing

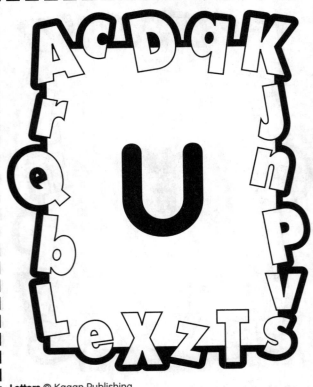

Letters © Kagan Publishing

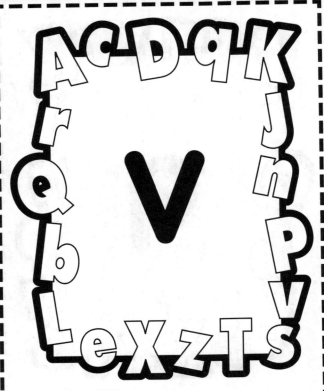

Letters © Kagan Publishing

Letters © Kagan Publishing

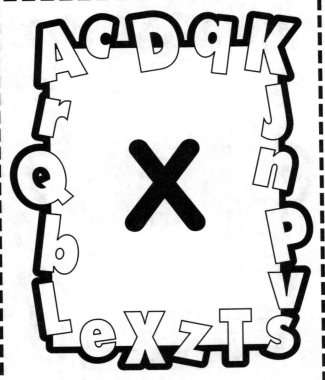

Letters © Kagan Publishing

Mix-N-Match: Primary
Kagan Publishing • 1 (800) 933-2667 • www.KaganOnline.com

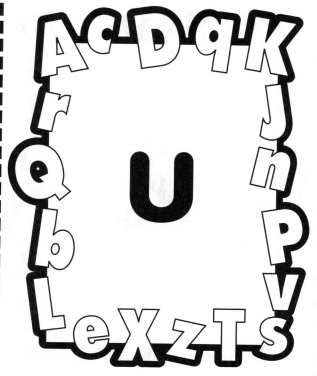

Letters © Kagan Publishing

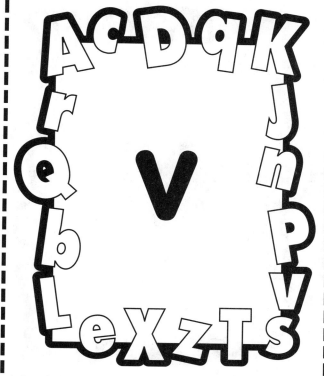

Letters © Kagan Publishing

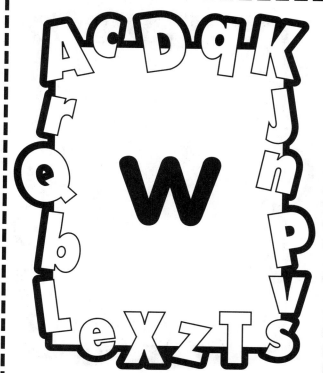

Letters © Kagan Publishing

Letters © Kagan Publishing

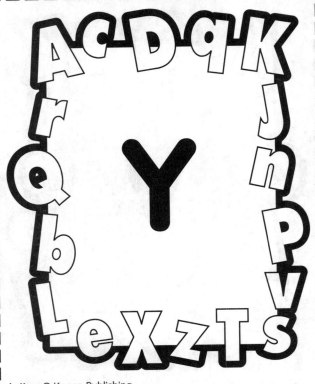

Letters © Kagan Publishing

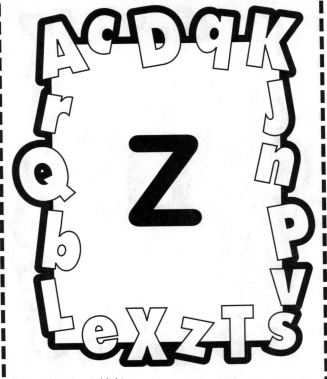

Letters © Kagan Publishing

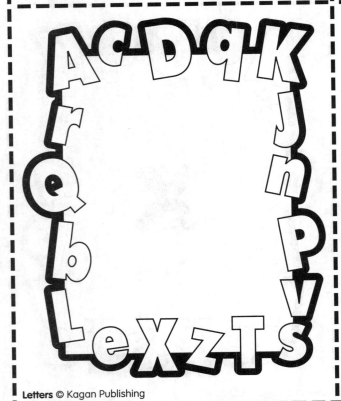

Letters © Kagan Publishing

Letters © Kagan Publishing

Mix-N-Match: Primary
Kagan Publishing • 1 (800) 933-2667 • www.KaganOnline.com

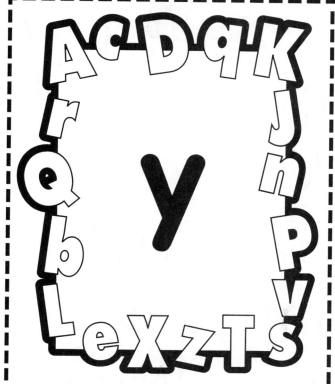

Letters © Kagan Publishing

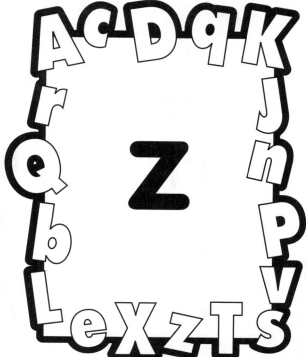

Letters © Kagan Publishing

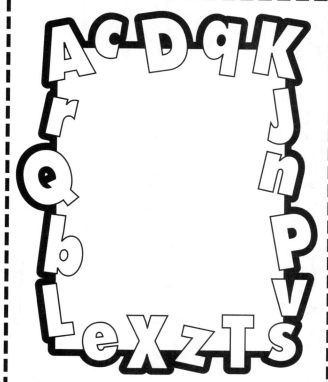

Letters © Kagan Publishing

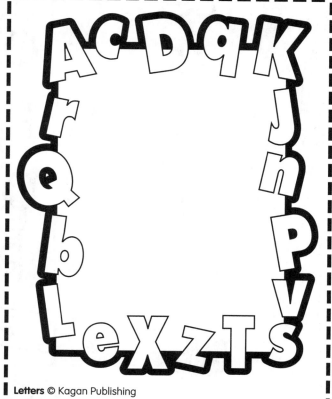

Letters © Kagan Publishing

The Alphabet
Upper and Lower Case Letters

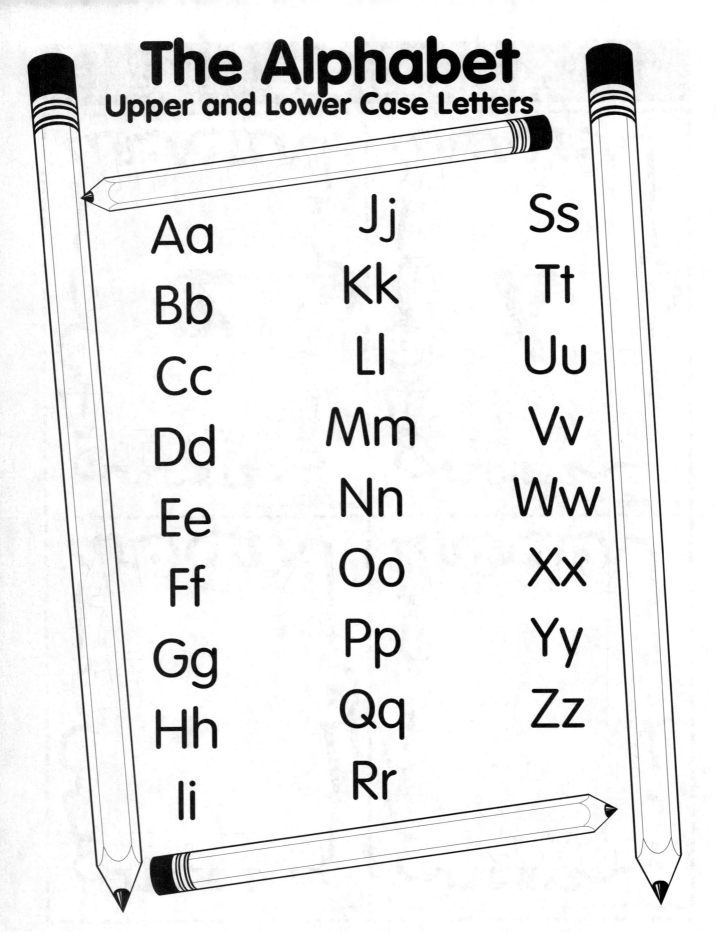

Aa

Bb

Cc

Dd

Ee

Ff

Gg

Hh

Ii

Jj

Kk

Ll

Mm

Nn

Oo

Pp

Qq

Rr

Ss

Tt

Uu

Vv

Ww

Xx

Yy

Zz

Mix-N-Match: Primary
Kagan Publishing • 1 (800) 933-2667 • www.KaganOnline.com

Numbers and Dots

Students practice connecting symbolic and concrete representations of numbers by matching number cards with dot cards.

Quizzing Questions

▶ **A Cards: Numbers**
- What number am I?
- Can you draw this many dots?

▶ **B Cards: Dots**
- What number am I?
- Can you draw this number?

Mix-N-Match: Primary
Kagan Publishing • 1 (800) 933-2667 • www.KaganOnline.com

Numbers and Dots

Draw the number of gumballs in the gumball machine.

19   **4**   **8**   **14**

9   **1**   **12**   **5**

2   **10**   **13**   **17**

Mix-N-Match: Primary
Kagan Publishing • 1 (800) 933-2667 • www.KaganOnline.com

Numbers and Dots

Write in the square the number of gumballs in the gumball machine.

Numbers and Dots

Numbers and Dots © Kagan Publishing

1

Numbers and Dots © Kagan Publishing

2

Numbers and Dots © Kagan Publishing

3

Numbers and Dots © Kagan Publishing

4

Mix-N-Match: Primary
Kagan Publishing • 1 (800) 933-2667 • www.KaganOnline.com

Numbers and Dots

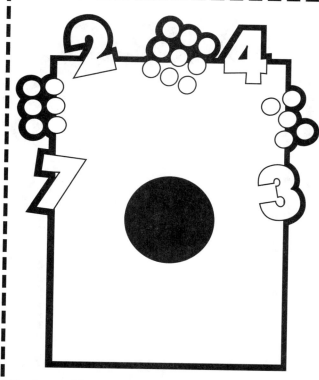

Numbers and Dots © Kagan Publishing

Numbers and Dots © Kagan Publishing

Numbers and Dots © Kagan Publishing

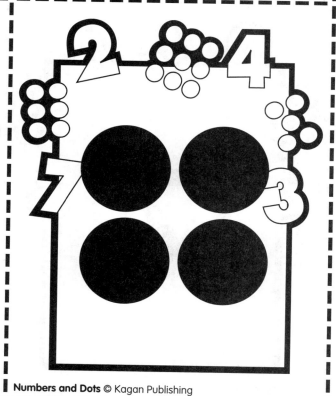

Numbers and Dots © Kagan Publishing

Numbers and Dots

Numbers and Dots © Kagan Publishing

Numbers and Dots © Kagan Publishing

Numbers and Dots © Kagan Publishing

Numbers and Dots © Kagan Publishing

Numbers and Dots

Numbers and Dots © Kagan Publishing

Numbers and Dots © Kagan Publishing

Numbers and Dots © Kagan Publishing

Numbers and Dots © Kagan Publishing

Numbers and Dots

Numbers and Dots © Kagan Publishing

Numbers and Dots © Kagan Publishing

Numbers and Dots © Kagan Publishing

Numbers and Dots © Kagan Publishing

Numbers and Dots

Numbers and Dots © Kagan Publishing

Numbers and Dots © Kagan Publishing

Numbers and Dots © Kagan Publishing

Numbers and Dots © Kagan Publishing

Numbers and Dots

Numbers and Dots © Kagan Publishing

Numbers and Dots © Kagan Publishing

Numbers and Dots © Kagan Publishing

Numbers and Dots © Kagan Publishing

Mix-N-Match: Primary

Kagan Publishing • 1 (800) 933-2667 • www.KaganOnline.com

Numbers and Dots

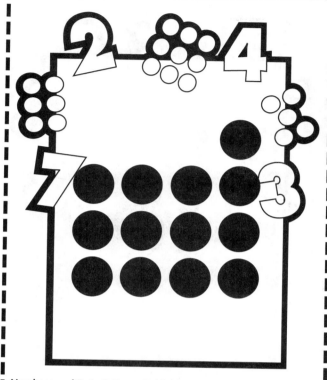

Numbers and Dots © Kagan Publishing

Numbers and Dots © Kagan Publishing

Numbers and Dots © Kagan Publishing

Numbers and Dots © Kagan Publishing

Numbers and Dots

17

Numbers and Dots © Kagan Publishing

18

Numbers and Dots © Kagan Publishing

19

Numbers and Dots © Kagan Publishing

20

Numbers and Dots © Kagan Publishing

Mix-N-Match: Primary
Kagan Publishing • 1 (800) 933-2667 • www.KaganOnline.com

Numbers and Dots

Numbers and Dots © Kagan Publishing

Numbers and Dots © Kagan Publishing

Numbers and Dots © Kagan Publishing

Numbers and Dots © Kagan Publishing

Numbers and Dots

1	**2**	**3**	**4**
5	**6**	**7**	**8**
9	**10**	**11**	**12**
13	**14**	**15**	**16**
17	**18**	**19**	**20**

Mix-N-Match: Primary

Kagan Publishing • 1 (800) 933-2667 • www.KaganOnline.com

Ordinal Numbers

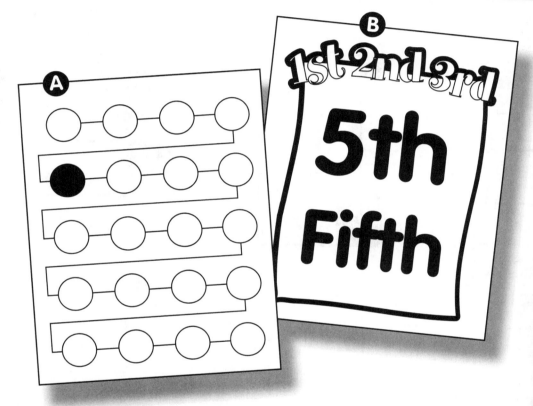

Students practice ordinal numbers by matching the picture card with its written ordinal number.

Quizzing Questions

► **A Cards: Ordinal Number Illustrations**
  • What place am I?
  • Where would your number be on my card?
► **B Cards: Written Ordinal Numbers**
  • What place am I?

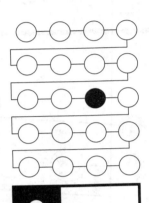

Ordinal Numbers

Write the ordinal number shown in the box.

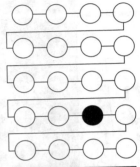

1 ☐

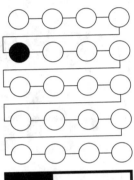

2 ☐

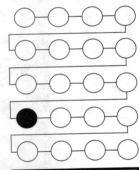

3 ☐

4 ☐

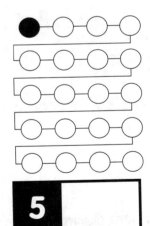

5 ☐

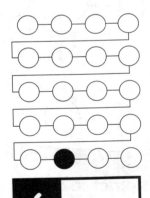

6 ☐

Mix-N-Match: Primary
Kagan Publishing • 1 (800) 933-2667 • www.KaganOnline.com

Ordinal Numbers

Color in the ordinal number indicated.

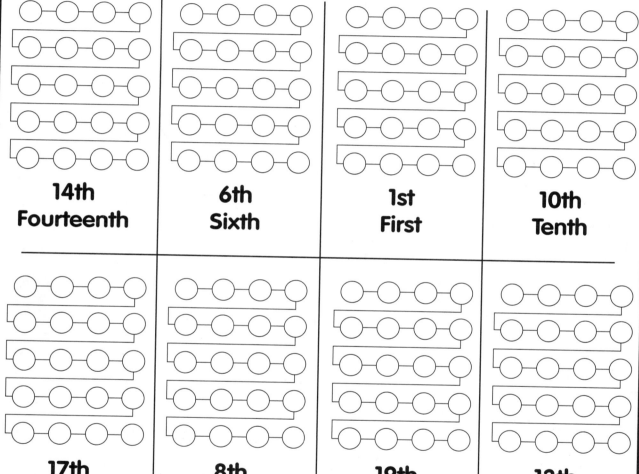

14th Fourteenth	**6th** Sixth	**1st** First	**10th** Tenth
17th Seventeenth	**8th** Eighth	**19th** Nineteenth	**13th** Thirteenth

Ordinal Numbers

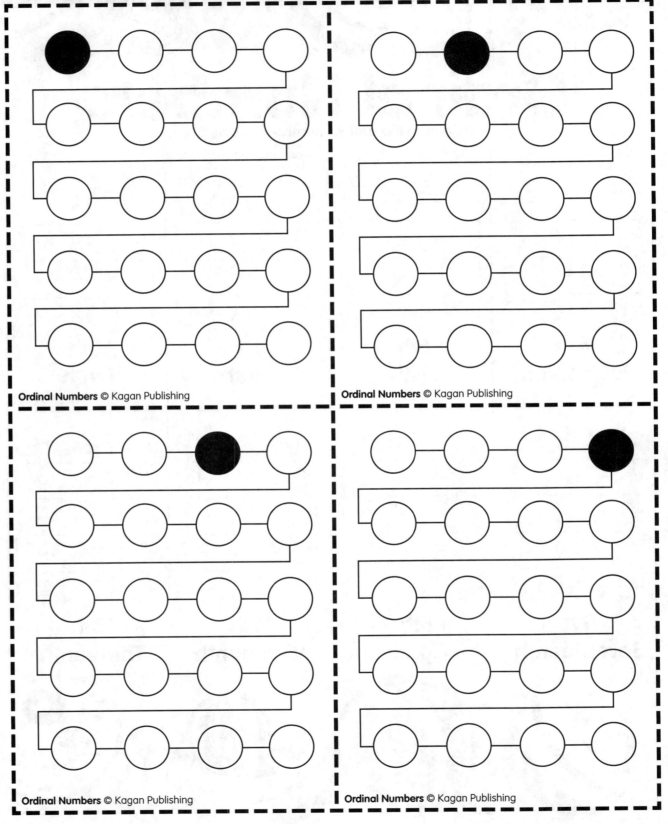

Ordinal Numbers © Kagan Publishing

Ordinal Numbers © Kagan Publishing

Ordinal Numbers © Kagan Publishing

Ordinal Numbers © Kagan Publishing

Ordinal Numbers

1st
First

Ordinal Numbers © Kagan Publishing

2nd
Second

Ordinal Numbers © Kagan Publishing

3rd
Third

Ordinal Numbers © Kagan Publishing

4th
Fourth

Ordinal Numbers © Kagan Publishing

Ordinal Numbers

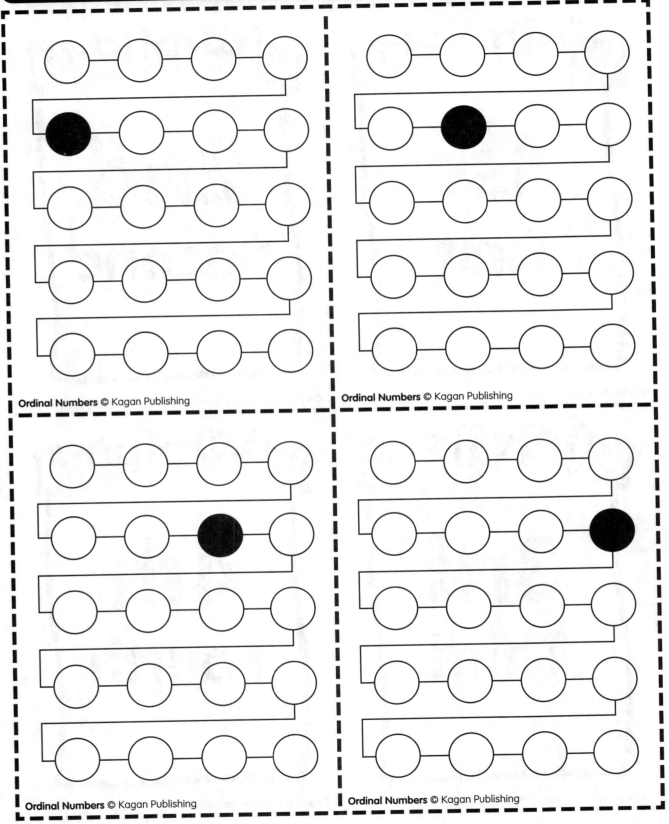

Ordinal Numbers © Kagan Publishing

Ordinal Numbers © Kagan Publishing

Ordinal Numbers © Kagan Publishing

Ordinal Numbers © Kagan Publishing

Mix-N-Match: Primary

Kagan Publishing • 1 (800) 933-2667 • www.KaganOnline.com

Ordinal Numbers

5th
Fifth

Ordinal Numbers © Kagan Publishing

1st 2nd 3rd

6th
Sixth

Ordinal Numbers © Kagan Publishing

7th
Seventh

Ordinal Numbers © Kagan Publishing

8th
Eighth

Ordinal Numbers © Kagan Publishing

Ordinal Numbers

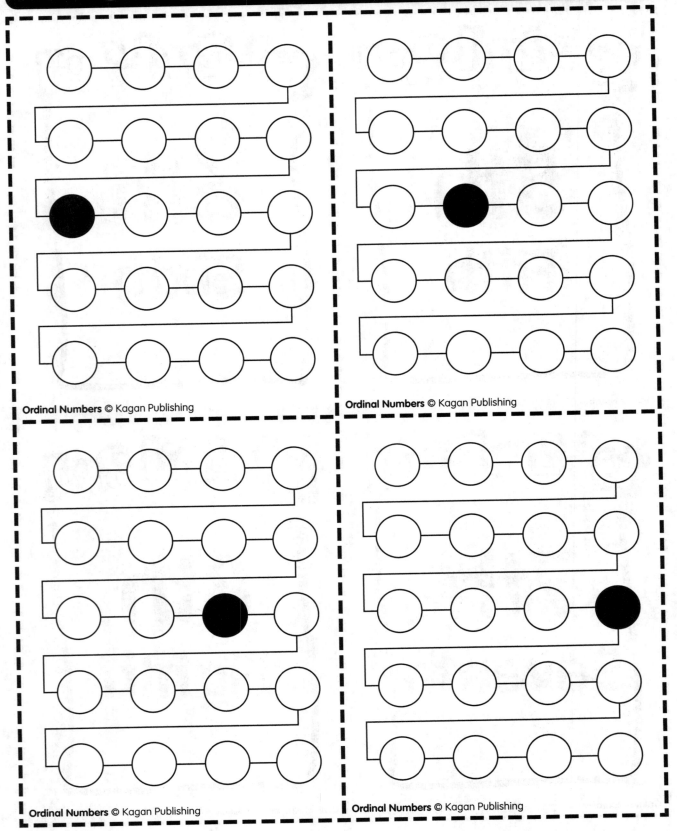

Ordinal Numbers © Kagan Publishing

Ordinal Numbers © Kagan Publishing

Ordinal Numbers © Kagan Publishing

Ordinal Numbers © Kagan Publishing

Mix-N-Match: Primary

Kagan Publishing • 1 (800) 933-2667 • www.KaganOnline.com

Ordinal Numbers

1st 2nd 3rd

9th
Ninth

Ordinal Numbers © Kagan Publishing

1st 2nd 3rd

10th
Tenth

Ordinal Numbers © Kagan Publishing

1st 2nd 3rd

11th
Eleventh

Ordinal Numbers © Kagan Publishing

1st 2nd 3rd

12th
Twelfth

Ordinal Numbers © Kagan Publishing

Ordinal Numbers

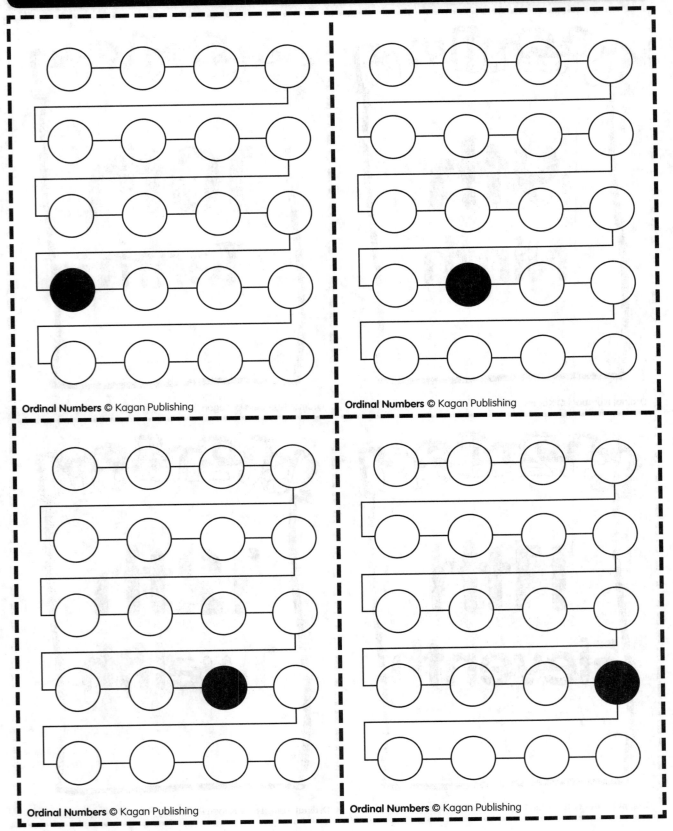

Ordinal Numbers © Kagan Publishing

Ordinal Numbers © Kagan Publishing

Ordinal Numbers © Kagan Publishing

Ordinal Numbers © Kagan Publishing

Mix-N-Match: Primary

Kagan Publishing • 1 (800) 933-2667 • www.KaganOnline.com

Ordinal Numbers

13th
Thirteenth

Ordinal Numbers © Kagan Publishing

14th
Fourteenth

Ordinal Numbers © Kagan Publishing

15th
Fifteenth

Ordinal Numbers © Kagan Publishing

16th
Sixteenth

Ordinal Numbers © Kagan Publishing

Ordinal Numbers

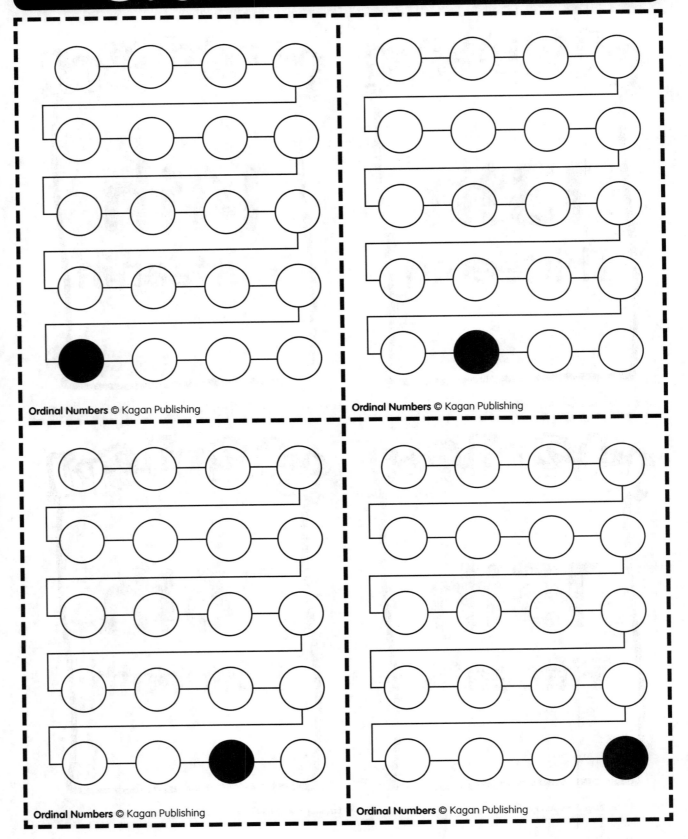

Ordinal Numbers © Kagan Publishing

Ordinal Numbers © Kagan Publishing

Ordinal Numbers © Kagan Publishing

Ordinal Numbers © Kagan Publishing

Ordinal Numbers

1st 2nd 3rd

17th
Seventeenth

Ordinal Numbers © Kagan Publishing

1st 2nd 3rd

18th
Eighteenth

Ordinal Numbers © Kagan Publishing

1st 2nd 3rd

19th
Nineteenth

Ordinal Numbers © Kagan Publishing

1st 2nd 3rd

20th
Twentieth

Ordinal Numbers © Kagan Publishing

Ordinal Numbers

First-1st	Second-2nd	Third-3rd	Fourth-4th

Fifth-5th	Sixth-6th	Seventh-7th	Eighth-8th

Ninth-9th	Tenth-10th	Eleventh-11th	Twelfth-12th

Thirteenth-13th	Fourteenth-14th	Fifteenth-15th	Sixteenth-16th

Seventeenth-17th	Eighteenth-18th	Nineteenth-19th	Twentieth-20th

Mix-N-Match: Primary
Kagan Publishing • 1 (800) 933-2667 • www.KaganOnline.com

Shapes

Students practice naming shapes by matching the shape to its name.

Quizzing Questions

▶ **A Cards: Shapes**
- What shape am I?
- Am I symmetrical?
- How many sides do I have?

▶ **B Cards: Shape Names**
- What do I look like?
- How many points do I have?

Shapes

Write the shape name in the blank.

1. _____	6. _____	11. _____	16. _____
2. _____	7. _____	12. _____	17. _____
3. _____	8. _____	13. _____	18. _____
4. _____	9. _____	14. _____	19. _____
5. _____	10. _____	15. _____	20. _____

Mix-N-Match: Primary

Kagan Publishing • 1 (800) 933-2667 • www.KaganOnline.com

Shapes

Draw the shape in the box.

1. Circle	6. Heart	11. Pentagon	16. Square
2. Crescent	7. Hexagon	12. Rectangle	17. Star
3. Cross	8. Line	13. Rhombus	18. Trapezoid
4. Decagon	9. Octagon	14. Semicircle	19. Triangle
5. Diamond	10. Oval	15. Spiral	20. Zigzag

Shapes © Kagan Publishing

Shapes © Kagan Publishing

Shapes © Kagan Publishing

Shapes © Kagan Publishing

Circle

Shapes © Kagan Publishing

Crescent

Shapes © Kagan Publishing

Cross

Shapes © Kagan Publishing

Decagon

Shapes © Kagan Publishing

Shapes

Shapes © Kagan Publishing

Shapes © Kagan Publishing

Shapes © Kagan Publishing

Shapes © Kagan Publishing

Mix-N-Match: Primary
Kagan Publishing • 1 (800) 933-2667 • www.KaganOnline.com

Shapes

Diamond

Heart

Hexagon

Line

Shapes © Kagan Publishing

Shapes © Kagan Publishing

Shapes © Kagan Publishing

Shapes © Kagan Publishing

Shapes

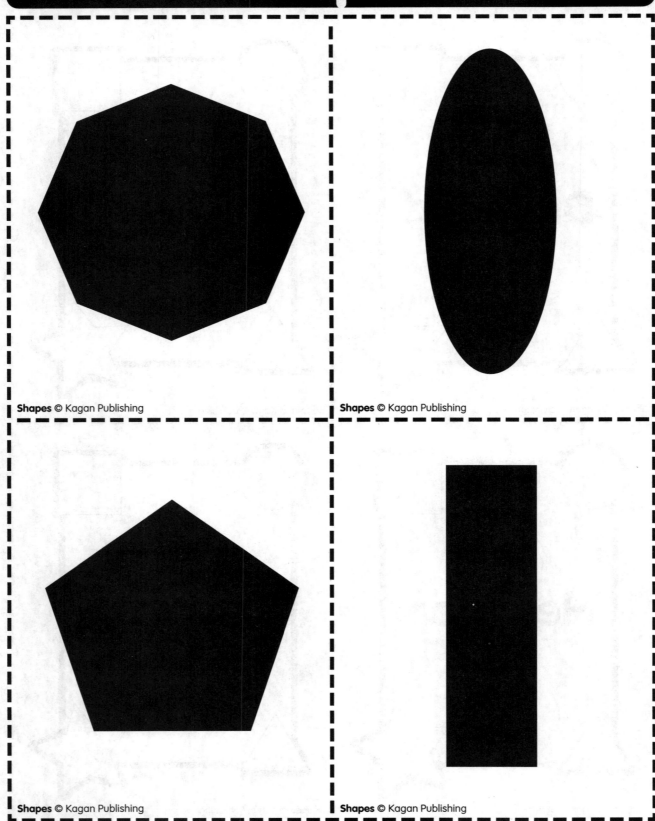

Shapes © Kagan Publishing

Shapes © Kagan Publishing

Shapes © Kagan Publishing

Shapes © Kagan Publishing

Mix-N-Match: Primary
Kagan Publishing • 1 (800) 933-2667 • www.KaganOnline.com

Octagon

Shapes © Kagan Publishing

Oval

Shapes © Kagan Publishing

Pentagon

Shapes © Kagan Publishing

Rectangle

Shapes © Kagan Publishing

Shapes

Shapes © Kagan Publishing

Shapes © Kagan Publishing

Shapes © Kagan Publishing

Shapes © Kagan Publishing

Mix-N-Match: Primary

Kagan Publishing • 1 (800) 933-2667 • www.KaganOnline.com

Shapes

Rhombus

Shapes © Kagan Publishing

Semicircle

Shapes © Kagan Publishing

Spiral

Shapes © Kagan Publishing

Square

Shapes © Kagan Publishing

Shapes

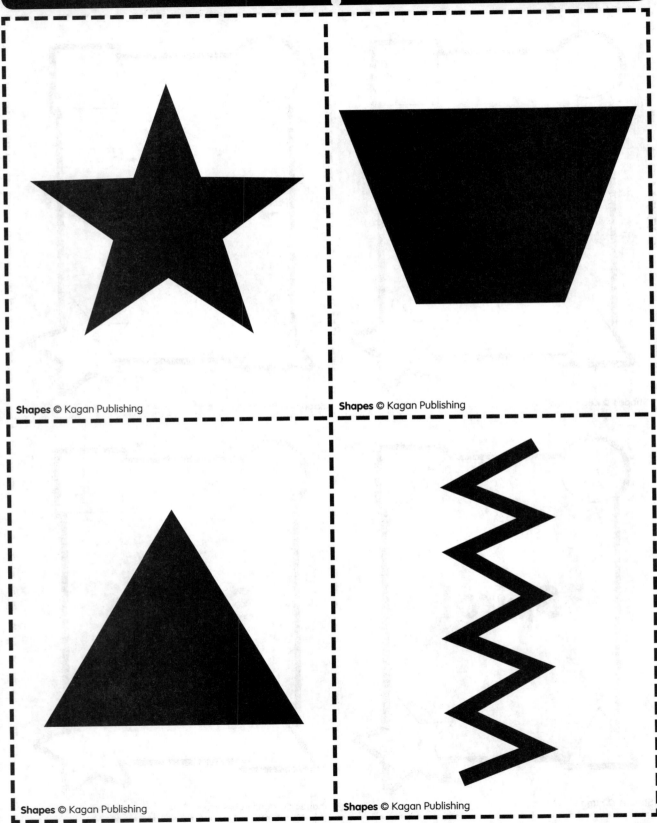

Shapes © Kagan Publishing

Shapes © Kagan Publishing

Shapes © Kagan Publishing

Shapes © Kagan Publishing

Shapes

Star

Shapes © Kagan Publishing

Trapezoid

Shapes © Kagan Publishing

Triangle

Shapes © Kagan Publishing

Zigzag

Shapes © Kagan Publishing

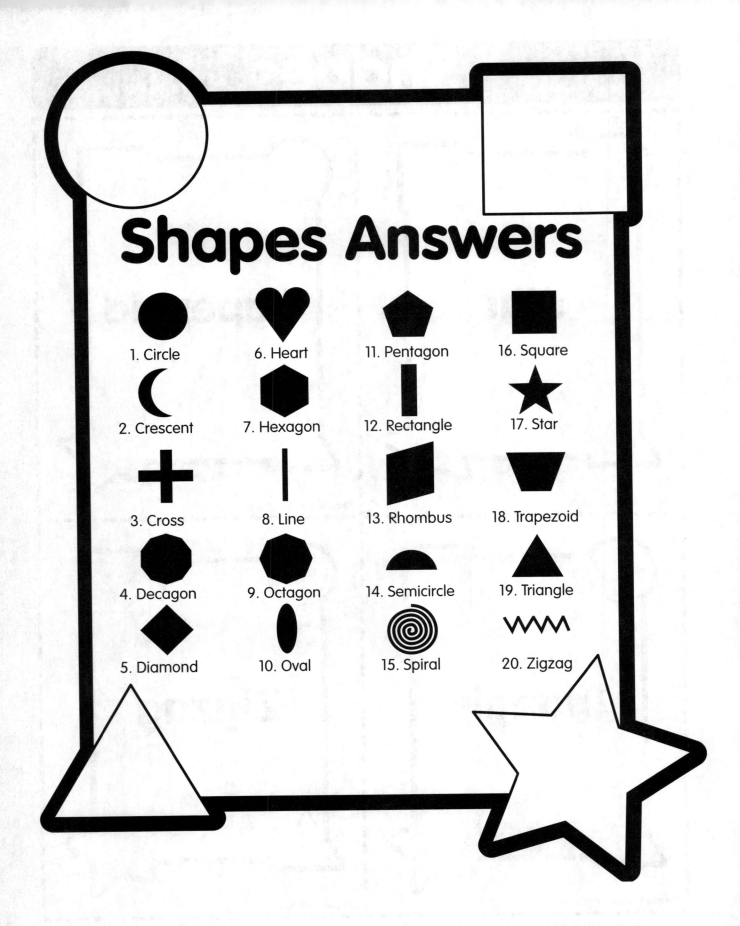

Shapes Answers

1. Circle
2. Crescent
3. Cross
4. Decagon
5. Diamond

6. Heart
7. Hexagon
8. Line
9. Octagon
10. Oval

11. Pentagon
12. Rectangle
13. Rhombus
14. Semicircle
15. Spiral

16. Square
17. Star
18. Trapezoid
19. Triangle
20. Zigzag

Mix-N-Match: Primary
Kagan Publishing • 1 (800) 933-2667 • www.KaganOnline.com

The Missing Letter

Students practice spelling by matching the illustrated word with the missing letter.

Quizzing Questions

▶ **A Cards: Words With a Letter Missing**
  • What letter am I missing?
▶ **B Cards: Missing Letters**
  • What is a word that begins with this letter?
  • What is a word that contains this letter?

The Missing Letter

Fill in the missing letter.

1. r___g

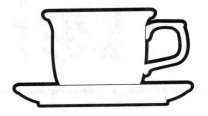

2. ___up

3. ___nt

4. ___og

5. ___aw

6. p___t

7. ___ar

8. su___

9. to___

Mix-N-Match: Primary
Kagan Publishing • 1 (800) 933-2667 • www.KaganOnline.com

The Missing Letter

Fill in the missing letter.

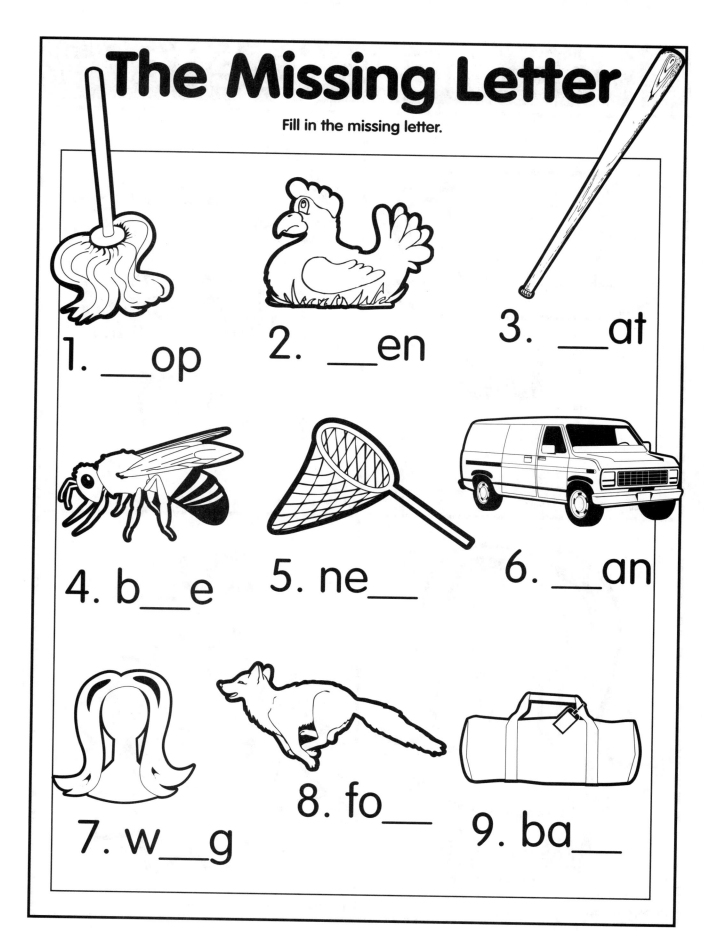

1. __op

2. __en

3. __at

4. b__e

5. ne__

6. __an

7. w__g

8. fo__

9. ba__

The Missing Letter

_up

_og

w_g

su_

The Missing Letter © Kagan Publishing

The Missing Letter © Kagan Publishing

The Missing Letter © Kagan Publishing

The Missing Letter © Kagan Publishing

Mix-N-Match: Primary
Kagan Publishing • 1 (800) 933-2667 • www.KaganOnline.com

The Missing Letter

The Missing Letter © Kagan Publishing

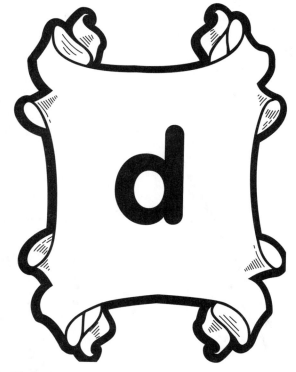

The Missing Letter © Kagan Publishing

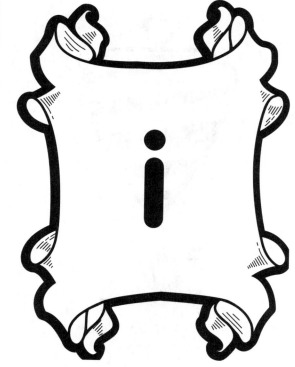

The Missing Letter © Kagan Publishing

The Missing Letter © Kagan Publishing

The Missing Letter

_at

_en

The Missing Letter © Kagan Publishing

The Missing Letter © Kagan Publishing

ne_

to_

The Missing Letter © Kagan Publishing

The Missing Letter © Kagan Publishing

Mix-N-Match: Primary
Kagan Publishing • 1 (800) 933-2667 • www.KaganOnline.com

The Missing Letter

The Missing Letter

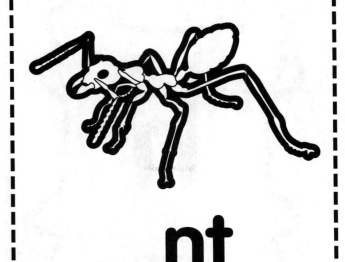

_nt

ba_

_un

p_t

The Missing Letter

The Missing Letter © Kagan Publishing

The Missing Letter © Kagan Publishing

The Missing Letter © Kagan Publishing

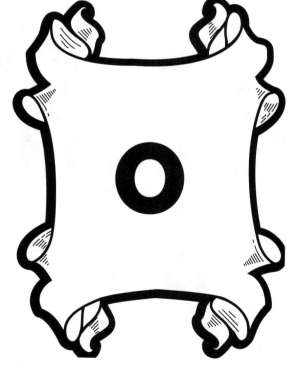

The Missing Letter © Kagan Publishing

The Missing Letter

_og

The Missing Letter © Kagan Publishing

_an

The Missing Letter © Kagan Publishing

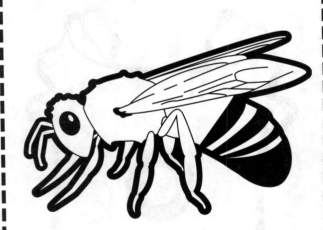

b_e

The Missing Letter © Kagan Publishing

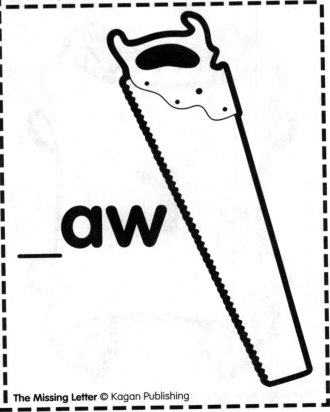

_aw

The Missing Letter © Kagan Publishing

Mix-N-Match: Primary
Kagan Publishing • 1 (800) 933-2667 • www.KaganOnline.com

The Missing Letter

The Missing Letter © Kagan Publishing

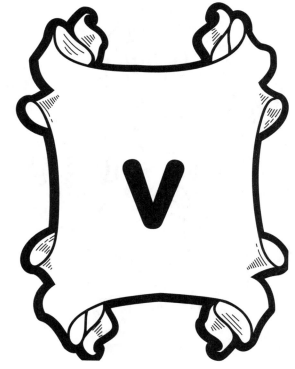

The Missing Letter © Kagan Publishing

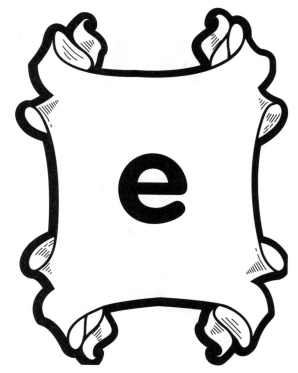

The Missing Letter © Kagan Publishing

The Missing Letter © Kagan Publishing

The Missing Letter

fo_

r_g

_op

_ar

The Missing Letter © Kagan Publishing

The Missing Letter © Kagan Publishing

The Missing Letter © Kagan Publishing

The Missing Letter © Kagan Publishing

Mix-N-Match: Primary

Kagan Publishing • 1 (800) 933-2667 • www.KaganOnline.com

The Missing Letter

The Missing Letter © Kagan Publishing

The Missing Letter © Kagan Publishing

The Missing Letter © Kagan Publishing

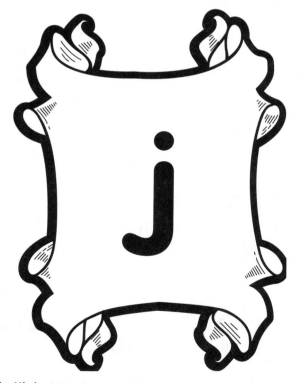

The Missing Letter © Kagan Publishing

The Missing Letter

 1. <u>c</u>up

 8. to<u>p</u>

 15. b<u>e</u>e

 2. <u>d</u>og

 9. <u>a</u>nt

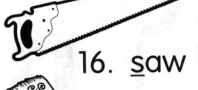 16. <u>s</u>aw

 3.wi<u>g</u>

 10. ba<u>g</u>

 17. r<u>u</u>g

 4. su<u>n</u>

 11. <u>r</u>un

 18. fo<u>x</u>

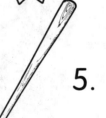 5. ba<u>t</u>

 12. p<u>o</u>t

 19.<u>m</u>op

 6. <u>h</u>en

 13. <u>l</u>og

20. <u>j</u>ar

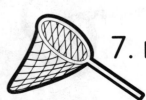 7. ne<u>t</u>

 14. <u>v</u>an

Mix-N-Match: Primary
Kagan Publishing • 1 (800) 933-2667 • www.KaganOnline.com

Transportation

Students learn about transportation by matching the vehicle with where it is used (land, water or air).

Quizzing Questions

▶ **A Cards: Vehicles**
- What am I?
- Do I travel by land, water, or air?

▶ **B Cards: Land, Water or Air**
- What is a vehicle that travels this way?

Transportation

Draw a line connecting the vehicle to where it is used (land, water, or air).

Land

Water

Air

Mix-N-Match: Primary

Kagan Publishing • 1 (800) 933-2667 • www.KaganOnline.com

Transportation

Draw a line connecting the vehicle to where it is used (land, water, or air).

Land

Water

Air

Transportation

Trolley

Transportation © Kagan Publishing

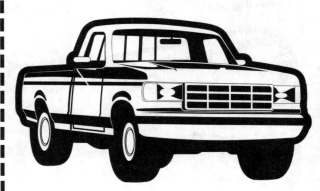

Truck

Transportation © Kagan Publishing

Van

Transportation © Kagan Publishing

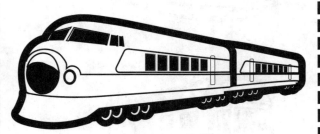

Train

Transportation © Kagan Publishing

Land

Transportation © Kagan Publishing

Land

Transportation © Kagan Publishing

Land

Transportation © Kagan Publishing

Land

Transportation © Kagan Publishing

Transportation

Motorcycle

Transportation © Kagan Publishing

Dirt Bike

Transportation © Kagan Publishing

Car

Transportation © Kagan Publishing

Bicycle

Transportation © Kagan Publishing

Mix-N-Match: Primary

Kagan Publishing • 1 (800) 933-2667 • www.KaganOnline.com

Land

Transportation © Kagan Publishing

Land

Transportation © Kagan Publishing

Land

Transportation © Kagan Publishing

Land

Transportation © Kagan Publishing

Transportation

Bus

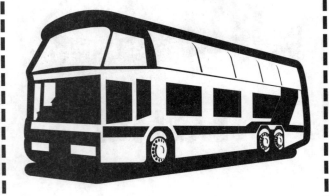

Snowmobile

Submarine

Rowboat

Land

Land

Transportation © Kagan Publishing

Transportation © Kagan Publishing

Water

Water

Transportation © Kagan Publishing

Transportation © Kagan Publishing

Transportation

Jet Ski

Motorboat

Sailboat

Kayak

Transportation © Kagan Publishing

Transportation © Kagan Publishing

Transportation © Kagan Publishing

Transportation © Kagan Publishing

Mix-N-Match: Primary
Kagan Publishing • 1 (800) 933-2667 • www.KaganOnline.com

Water

Transportation © Kagan Publishing

Water

Transportation © Kagan Publishing

Water

Transportation © Kagan Publishing

Water

Transportation © Kagan Publishing

Transportation

Helicopter

Transportation © Kagan Publishing

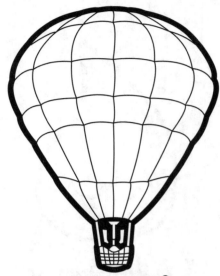

Hot Air Balloon

Transportation © Kagan Publishing

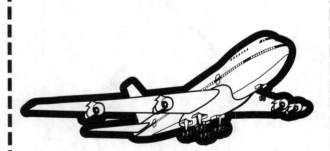

Airplane

Transportation © Kagan Publishing

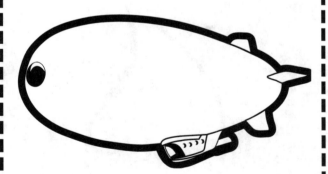

Blimp

Transportation © Kagan Publishing

Air

Transportation © Kagan Publishing

Air

Transportation © Kagan Publishing

Air

Transportation © Kagan Publishing

Air

Transportation © Kagan Publishing

Transportation

Land

Water

Air

Mix-N-Match: Primary

Kagan Publishing • 1 (800) 933-2667 • www.KaganOnline.com

MIX-N-MATCH
NOTES

MASTERING CONTENT HAS NEVER BEEN MORE FUN!

REPRODUCIBLE MIX-N-MATCH CARDS & ACTIVITIES

★ LANGUAGE ARTS
★ MATHEMATICS
★ PRIMARY
★ SCIENCE
★ SOCIAL STUDIES

CALL FOR FREE CATALOGS!   *Kagan*   OR VISIT US ONLINE!

1 (800) 933-2667   WWW.KAGANONLINE.COM

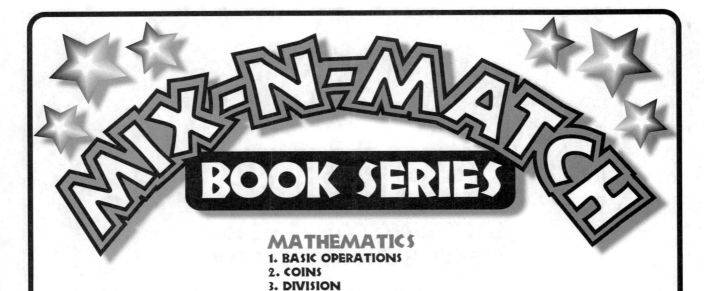

MIX-N-MATCH

BOOK SERIES

MATHEMATICS
1. BASIC OPERATIONS
2. COINS
3. DIVISION
4. EQUIVALENT FRACTIONS
5. FRACTIONS AND PERCENTS
6. GRAPHING ORDERED PAIRS
7. MEASUREMENT CONVERSIONS
8. MULTIPLICATION
9. PLACE VALUE
10. READING TIME
11. ROMAN NUMERALS
12. SUBTRACTION

LANGUAGE ARTS
1. ABBREVIATIONS
2. ANTONYMS
3. CLASSIFYING NOUNS
4. COMPOUND WORDS
5. CONTRACTIONS
6. DICTIONARY GUIDE WORDS
7. DOUBLE LETTER SPELLING WORDS
8. FACT OR OPINION
9. HOMONYMS
10. PARTS OF SPEECH
11. PREFIXES
12. SYNONYMS

SOCIAL STUDIES
1. FAMOUS AMERICANS
2. FAMOUS PLACES
3. FIRE SAFETY
4. GEOGRAPHY VOCABULARY
5. HISTORICAL EVENTS
6. HOLIDAYS
7. INVENTIONS
8. LANDFORMS
9. STATE GEOGRAPHY
10. STATES AND CAPITALS
11. THE BILL OF RIGHTS
12. WORLD GEOGRAPHY

LOOK WHAT'S INSIDE!

PRIMARY
1. ADDITION
2. ANIMALS
3. BEGINNING CONSONANTS AND VOWELS
4. COMMUNITY HELPERS
5. FOOD
6. LESS THAN, GREATER THAN
7. LETTERS
8. NUMBERS AND DOTS
9. ORDINAL NUMBERS
10. SHAPES
11. THE MISSING LETTER
12. TRANSPORTATION

SCIENCE
1. ANIMAL ADULT AND BABY NAMES
2. ANIMAL CLASSIFICATION
3. BODY PARTS
4. BUGS AND INSECTS
5. CELL ANATOMY
6. EXPLORING SPACE VOCABULARY
7. HUMAN BODY FUN FACTS
8. HUMAN BODY SYSTEMS
9. MATTER AND ENERGY VOCABULARY
10. OCEAN LIFE
11. THE FOOD PYRAMID
12. WEATHER VOCABULARY

CALL FOR FREE CATALOGS!   *Kagan*   **OR VISIT US ONLINE!**

1 (800) 933-2667   WWW.KAGANONLINE.COM

Kagan

It's All About Engagement!

Kagan is the world leader

in creating active engagement in the classroom. Learn how to engage your students and you will boost achievement, prevent discipline problems, and make learning more fun and meaningful. Come join Kagan for a workshop or call Kagan to **set up a workshop for your school or district**. Experience the power of a Kagan workshop. **Experience the engagement!**

SPECIALIZING IN:

- ★ **Cooperative Learning**
- ★ **Win-Win Discipline**
- ★ **Brain-Friendly Teaching**
- ★ **Multiple Intelligences**
- ★ **Thinking Skills**
- ★ **Kagan Coaching**

KAGAN PROFESSIONAL DEVELOPMENT

www.KaganOnline.com ★ 1(800) 266-7576

Kagan

It's All About Engagement!

Kagan is your source
for active engagement in the classroom.

Check out Kagan's line of books, SmartCards, software, electronics, and hands-on learning resources—all designed to boost engagement in your classroom.

Books

SmartCards

Spinners

Learning Chips

Posters

Learning Cubes

KAGAN PUBLISHING

www.KaganOnline.com ★ 1(800) 933-2667